TO:

_____

FROM:

_____

DATE:

_____

# Praise for *The Anne of Green Gables Devotional*

"Rachel Dodge's devotional is not only a chapter-by-chapter companion to *Anne of Green Gables* but also a day-by-day companion to the modern reader seeking encouragement, enlightenment, and holy scope for the imagination. An absolute joy to be immersed in the deep, abiding roots of kindred spirit living."

–Sarah McCoy, *New York Times*, *USA Today*, and international bestselling author of *Marilla of Green Gables*

"Rejection, disappointment, loneliness—ways to cope with these and many other of life's challenges are highlighted in this book of devotionals drawn from L. M. Montgomery's classic *Anne of Green Gables*. 'Rich spiritual themes and truths' found in each of the thirty-eight chapters inspire and encourage us to find joy, beauty, and serenity in our own lives. A valuable addition to Anne collections everywhere."

–Carolyn Strom Collins, author of *The Anne of Green Gables Treasury*, *Anne of Green Gables: The Original Manuscript*, etc.

"This book is a treasure. I loved it! Rachel took some of our favorite moments in the classic Anne stories and infused them with deeper insights by pairing them with scripture. If this charmer of a devotion were a dress, it would have puffed sleeves. The puffiest."

–Robin Jones Gunn, author of the Haven Maker series and Christy Miller series

"*The Anne of Green Gables Devotional* is a delight from cover to cover! Rachel Dodge has filled its pages with beautifully crafted reflections and prayers inspired by the beloved novel. This is a stirring, timely devotional for all of us who seek to belong and yearn for our loving, forever home."

–Julie Klassen, author of the Tales From Ivy Hill series

"*The Anne of Green Gables Devotional* paints vividly on the canvas for us the subtle themes of faith, chapter-by-chapter, that are sprinkled throughout the beloved story of Anne Shirley. Kindred spirits, this is the scripture-based introspective book we've all been missing from our Anne collection and need to immediately add to our bookshelves!"

–Jen Smith, book collector, photographer, and curator
of Storybook Style (@storybookstyle)

"What a gift to Anne fans! Our favorite literary heroine has much to teach us about love and acceptance, and Rachel Dodge does a beautiful job unwrapping the complexities of Anne's story within the context of the greatest adoption story of all—showing us how we too can be transformed by the gift of true belonging."

–Jenny Williams, artist and owner of Carrot Top Paper Shop

"In this soul-rejuvenating book, Rachel Dodge takes these gleaming treasures out one by one and hands them to her readers."

–Lorilee Craker, author of 15 books, including *Anne of
Green Gables, My Daughter and Me: What My Favorite Book
Taught Me About Grace, Belonging and the Orphan in Us All;
Money Secrets of the Amish; Through the Storm* with Lynne
Spears; and *My Journey to Heaven* with Marv Besteman

"Heartwarming and truly inspired, a must-read for anyone who's ever felt rejected—that's all of us."

–Wendi Lou Lee, author of *A Prairie Devotional:
Inspired by the Beloved TV Series*

"This book is perfect for any age, including the young lady in your life who is meeting Anne for the first time. It is the perfect companion to a beloved book and is a wonderful gift for yourself and others!"

–Julie Fisk, co-author of *The One Year Daily Acts of Kindness
Devotional* and *The One Year Daily Acts of Friendship Devotional*

# The Anne of GREEN GABLES Devotional

### A Chapter-by-Chapter Companion
#### for Kindred Spirits

Rachel Dodge

## BARBOUR BOOKS
An Imprint of Barbour Publishing, Inc.

*To my loving family,*
*for their encouragement and support*

---

*It's a million times nicer to be*
*Anne of Green Gables than Anne*
*of nowhere in particular, isn't it?*

Anne Shirley

# Contents

# A Kindred Spirit Welcome

Reading and rereading *Anne of Green Gables* by L. M. Montgomery is a favorite tradition of mine—and I know I'm not alone. Anne Shirley's story of adoption and belonging has delighted generations of readers from around the world for over one hundred years. Set in the fictional town of Avonlea, against the picturesque backdrop of Prince Edward Island, *Anne of Green Gables* brims with charming characters and heartwarming moments.

Anne's story is beloved because it expresses some of life's most universal longings and assures us that goodness and beauty still exist in this world. Anne's character inspires us to love the loveless, see the good in others, give people second chances, dream big dreams, and embrace life with open arms. Her grit spurs us to press on through life's challenges. We understand her feelings of rejection and loneliness, her longing for a family and a home, and her many trials and tribulations. And our hearts swell when Anne finds what we all want most: unconditional love, a safe place to dream and grow, and the freedom to explore her place and purpose in the world.

*Anne of Green Gables* is also filled with rich spiritual themes and truths. Anne's story provides a gentle allegory for God's redemptive, adoptive plans for each of us. Not only is she adopted, as we are adopted into God's family when we place our trust in Jesus as our Savior, but she grows and flourishes in a loving family, just as we do as part of the body of Christ.

Even Anne's arrival at Green Gables—by a "queer mistake"—

is later recognized as a divine appointment. Matthew says, "She's been a blessing to us, and there never was a luckier mistake than what Mrs. Spencer made—if it was luck. I don't believe it was any such thing. It was Providence, because the Almighty saw we needed her, I reckon" (ch. 34). And Marilla tells Anne, "I don't know what I'd do if you weren't here—if you'd never come" (ch. 37).

Anne's own journey of faith is central to the plot as she learns to pray, attends church, goes to prayer meetings, sings in the choir, contemplates morality and theology, and practices curbing her temper. Early on, Marilla realizes Anne knows "nothing about God's love, since she had never had it translated to her through the medium of human love" (ch. 7); thus, much of the story centers on Anne's experience of human love and loyalty. Surrounded by wholesome friends, mentors, and role models, Anne's faith blossoms and her character develops.

Finally, Anne's story reminds us that God makes no mistakes. His thoughts are not like our thoughts; His ways are not like our ways (Isaiah 55:8). He's intimately involved and invested in our growth and well-being. God's plans for us are for our *good* (Jeremiah 29:11). He knows what we need far better than we do, and He gives us the desires of our hearts (Psalm 37:4).

———————— ✳ ————————

Kindred spirit, this book is your invitation to explore the spiritual themes in Anne's story and God's unique plans and purposes for your life as a child of God. It's designed as a devotional companion to *Anne of Green Gables*, with a corresponding devotional entry for each chapter of the book. Each entry includes key Bible verses, examples from the book, thoughts for personal application, and a short prayer. Several special features, including discussion questions, can be found at the back of the book. You can read this devotional on your own, with your family, in a group, or with a bosom friend.

As you sit down to read each day, picture yourself curled up in Anne's east gable room, looking out at the giant blossoming cherry tree. This is your quiet time with Jesus—a time when you can set aside life's trials and tribulations and breathe in God's healing love and acceptance. May this devotional nourish your soul and lead you into a deeper understanding of God's redemptive plans for your life.

*Note to parents: If you're reading this book with younger children, I've created a special set of supplemental application questions for kids that you can print out to go along with your daily readings. Please visit www.RachelDodge.com/anneforkids for more.

# Day 1
# A DIVINE DETOUR

*The mind of man plans his way,
but the LORD directs his steps.*
PROVERBS 16:9 NASB

> ## "Well, we're not getting a girl."
>
> (CH. 1)

When Marilla Cuthbert says this to Mrs. Rachel Lynde, her well-meaning, busybody neighbor, she has no idea what (or who) is coming her way. She's preparing to welcome a "desired and expected" young boy into her home, "old enough to be of some use in doing chores. . .and young enough to be trained up proper." She's anticipating a practical solution to a pressing problem: Matthew is getting on in years, his heart troubles him, and they need help on the farm.

In this chapter Marilla expects several things. She expects Mrs. Lynde's visit: "She had known that the sight of Matthew jaunting off so unaccountably would be too much for her neighbor's curiosity." She expects Matthew and the new boy home in time to eat: she has set the table for three. And she expects the boy to sleep in the kitchen: she has prepared a simple "couch" for him there.

Marilla is *not* expecting her carefully ordered life to turn upside down. Though she's planning to give the boy "a good home and schooling," she's completely unprepared for motherhood. Anne's arrival opens a new world to Marilla and satisfies a longing buried deep in her heart. Soon enough, she and Matthew both realize that the "queer mistake" that landed Anne at Green Gables is actually a blessing. Matthew credits "the Almighty" for sending Anne because He saw that they "needed her" (ch. 34). And Anne becomes Marilla's "joy and comfort" (ch. 37).

Marilla's best-laid plans didn't go as expected. She and Matthew thought they needed an extra pair of hands around the farm, but God knew they needed a daughter. Often God's plans for us are unexpected. We anticipate one thing, and something else—or someone else—shows up instead. We plan, make schedules and lists, do our part to get the ball rolling, and then something akin to a girl instead of a boy comes waltzing into our lives.

God is not surprised by our detours and delays. He works in and through them in divine ways. Proverbs 16:9 reminds us of God's promise to direct and establish our steps. We can and should make plans, but God is ultimately in charge. When you allow Him to direct your life, He brings about things beyond your imagination. His plans for you are for your good—not to harm you but to prosper you (Jeremiah 29:11). We're told in Romans 8:28 that God works for the good of those who love Him. He sees the big picture of your life, and nothing surprises Him.

*O the depth of the riches both of the wisdom*
*and knowledge of God! how unsearchable are his*
*judgments, and his ways past finding out!*
Romans 11:33 kjv

## PERSONAL APPLICATION:

This opening scene in the Green Gables kitchen points us to an important reminder: God often gives us what we don't know we need. As you make plans, invite God to make revisions. If you're prone to making hasty decisions, pray and give God space and time to lead you forward. If you find yourself on a divine detour, ask the Holy Spirit to open your eyes to God's bigger plans for you. He may have something in mind that you can't yet imagine.

Is there someone in your life who needs encouragement? Someone facing an unexpected twist or turn? Someone with a broken heart? Take a few minutes to make a call or send a note this week. Share Proverbs 16:9 and Jeremiah 29:11 and remind him or her of God's loving plans.

## PRAYER FOR TODAY:

*Lord, thank You for directing and establishing
my steps. I lay all of my best-laid plans at Your feet.
I need Your wisdom and guidance to navigate the
unexpected circumstances in my life. Help me to see
Your purposes in the detours and delays I'm currently
facing, and show me the right way to go. [Add your
prayer request.] In Jesus' name, amen.*

---

*"For I know the plans I have for you," declares
the LORD, "plans to prosper you and not to harm you,
plans to give you hope and a future."*
JEREMIAH 29:11 NIV

# Day 2
# SOMEONE TO LISTEN

*The eyes of the LORD are on the righteous,
and his ears are attentive to their cry.*
PSALM 34:15 NIV

> "You can talk as much as
> you like. I don't mind."
>
> (CH. 2)

When Matthew Cuthbert says these words to Anne after she chatters away for most of their buggy ride from the train station to Green Gables, it's music to her ears. All her life Anne has been told to settle down, hold her tongue, and stop prattling on. Anne says, "People are always telling me I [talk too much]." Mrs. Spencer thinks Anne's tongue must be "hung in the middle." Anne claims she can stop talking if she tries hard enough, but Matthew tells Anne she can talk as much as she likes.

As they drive, Matthew is surprised to find he "kind of like[s] her chatter." A shy man of few words, Matthew is glad when someone else carries the conversation. He normally feels nervous around "the Avonlea type of well-bred little girl," but he likes Anne's way of talking. And though he "never expected to enjoy the society of a little girl," he enjoys Anne's "big ideas" and the "big words" she uses to express them. He listens to her darting thoughts with interest.

This scene marks the beginning of Anne and Matthew's poignant father-daughter relationship. Matthew is most likely the first person who has ever truly listened to Anne. He doesn't find her alarming or strange. He doesn't mind what Mrs. Lynde later refers to as Anne's "queer way of expressing herself" (ch. 10). He enjoys her company. In fact, her unique quirks—the things that make her different from the other girls—are what endear her to him most. He likes her just the way she is.

Matthew delights in Anne's personality, in her view of the world, in her imagination, and in her way of talking. To an even greater degree, God delights in you and the way He made you. He loves your talents, your abilities, your spunk, your thoughts, the way you speak, and the way you notice the needs of others. He likes the way you look at the world and express yourself. He looks at what's on the inside—not at your appearance—and sees your heart.

With God you can talk as much as you like. When you pray, He leans in and listens with understanding. He is attentive to your prayers (Psalm 34:15). He invites you to come to Him with everything—your hopes and dreams, joys and concerns; your ideas and plans, worries and anxieties; and your temptations and difficulties, sorrows and pains. Your prayer is "His delight" (Proverbs 15:8 NASB). God never tires of hearing from you; in fact, He invites you to "pray without ceasing" (1 Thessalonians 5:17 KJV). He wants you to enjoy deep, ongoing fellowship with Him.

*The prayer of the upright is His delight.*
PROVERBS 15:8 NASB

## Personal Application:

Do you long for someone who will listen to you and understand you? Anne felt lonely and misunderstood for much of her young life, but Matthew took time to listen to what she had to say. Be assured that Jesus knows you, loves you, and is interested in you and your concerns. He understands what you're going through. Take this time to pour out your heart to the Lord and tell Him everything.

Do you know someone who needs a listening ear? Pray about ways you can reach out to the lonely, the overlooked, or the misunderstood people in your life. A small act of kindness, a note of encouragement, or a friend to talk to can go a long way toward helping someone feel loved and valued.

## Prayer for Today:

*Lord, thank You for loving me so well. Thank You
for listening to me and for delighting in my prayers.
I want to enjoy sweet fellowship with You and talk to
You like a best friend and loving father. Please remind
me to draw close to You in prayer all day today.
Help me to be a better listener in my relationships.
[Add your prayer request.] In Jesus' name, amen.*

---

*Though my father and mother forsake me,
the Lord will receive me.*
Psalm 27:10 niv

# Day 3
# COMFORT IN DISTRESS

———————————— ✳ ————————————

*The Lord is close to the brokenhearted*
*and saves those who are crushed in spirit.*
PSALM 34:18 NIV

> "You don't want me because I'm not a boy!
> I might have expected it. Nobody ever did
> want me. I might have known it was all too
> beautiful to last. I might have known
> nobody really did want me." (CH. 3)

After saying this, Anne sits down, buries her face in her arms, and bursts into tears. Matthew and Marilla are bewildered and shocked at Anne's arrival and have no idea how to comfort her. Marilla lamely tells her not to cry, that there's no need for tears. Anne violently disagrees, saying, "You would cry, too, if you were an orphan and had come to a place you thought was going to be home and found that they didn't want you because you weren't a boy."

In this chapter, Anne comes face-to-face with the bitter reality that she's not wanted. Her dreams of a home and family come to a screeching halt as she realizes there's been a terrible, heart-shattering mistake. The days and nights of waiting to meet Matthew and Marilla, the exciting train ride to Avonlea, the glory of the buggy ride with Matthew, the Lake of Shining Waters and White Way Delight, and the first glimpse of beautiful Green Gables all come to an abrupt end. Every wish she thought was coming true is gone.

Anne's words express the heartrending pain of a life of rejection. She tells her entire life story with the simple phrase "Nobody ever did want me." With five words, we learn that she has never been loved or cared for. No one has ever invited her in or made her feel welcome. She has been lonely and soul-starved for as long as she can remember. And just when she thinks things are going to get better, everything falls apart.

It's difficult to read this chapter because Anne's pain is so vivid—and so familiar. Not everyone knows what it feels like to be orphaned or abandoned, but most of us have experienced the crushing reality of rejection in one way or another. We all know what it's like to be unwanted, uninvited, or ignored. We've seen treasured hopes and dreams shatter. And often the people around us don't know how to provide the comfort we need.

With God we find the compassion and understanding we crave in times of distress. Psalm 34:18 (NIV) gives us a wonderful promise: "The LORD is close to the brokenhearted and saves those who are crushed in spirit." He knows every bit of rejection you've faced in your life; He knows every hurt, every cruel word, every stab. He is with you, and He understands you. Jesus can relate to your pain uniquely because He too experienced deep rejection and sorrow.

*He is despised and rejected by men,*
*a Man of sorrows and acquainted with grief.*
ISAIAH 53:3 NKJV

## PERSONAL APPLICATION:

We've all felt abandoned, unwanted, or alone. We know the pain that comes with rejection. When there's no one else who understands and no one who can help, God never leaves our side. When we're hurting, He acts as a shelter and a hiding place. When we're in need, he is there: "God is our refuge and strength, a very present help in trouble" (Psalm 46:1 KJV).

Do you know someone who is facing heartache or rejection? The Lord wants to use you to share His love and comfort in practical ways. Showing up for someone doesn't have to be complicated. A hug, a note, or a flower from your garden all show you understand and care.

## PRAYER FOR TODAY:

*God of all comfort, I lift up to You the pain and rejection I've experienced. I take refuge in You now. Thank You that You are near to me in my distress. I believe You have the power to heal the wounded places of my heart. I invite You to bind up what's broken and comfort me in this area of my life. [Add your prayer request.] In Jesus' name, amen.*

---※---

*Blessed be the God and Father of our Lord Jesus Christ, the Father of mercies and God of all comfort, who comforts us in all our affliction.*
2 CORINTHIANS 1:3-4 ESV

# Day 4
# DEFENDER OF THE WEAK

*A father to the fatherless, a defender of*
*widows, is God in his holy dwelling.*
*God sets the lonely in families.*
PSALM 68:5-6 NIV

> "It's easier to be cheerful
> and bear up under affliction
> on a sunshiny day." (CH. 4)

Anne tries to make the best of her first morning at Green Gables, even though it's most likely her last. She glories in the beauty of Green Gables with its "showers" of flower blossoms, "dizzily sweet fragrance[s]," "green, low-sloping fields," large barns, "sparkling blue glimpse of sea," and "delightful possibilities," but she knows it's not for her. She tries to remain cheerful and "bear up" under her affliction, all while her heart is breaking.

The life Anne wants most is right in front of her—just out of reach. By nightfall she will most likely be in yet another house in yet another bed. Anne believes she has no friend, no one on her side, no one who wants her. She feels rejected, hopeless, and alone. The previous chapter ends with this heartrending sentence: "And up-stairs, in the east gable, a lonely, heart-hungry, friendless child cried herself to sleep" (ch. 3).

In this scene, Anne is yet unaware of any change in her circumstances. She doesn't know that something shifted during the night, that after she cried herself to sleep—feeling friendless and alone—a softhearted, kindly old bachelor spoke up and said he wanted her. While Anne slept, Marilla made plans to take Anne back, but Matthew quietly put his foot down. Marilla said no, but Matthew stubbornly said yes. Marilla asked, "What good would she be to us?" And Matthew answered, "We might be some good to her."

Matthew's quiet intervention is a picture of God's work in our lives, for our salvation and for our good. God is a "father to the fatherless" who "sets the lonely in families" (Psalm 68:6 NIV). Before we knew Him, He knew us. When we were powerless to save ourselves, He intervened. While we were "still sinners, Christ died for us" (Romans 5:8 NIV). God invites each of us into His own family through faith in Christ, that we might know God personally and become children of God (John 1:12).

In the New Testament, Jesus stepped in and changed the course of innumerable lives. To the crippled man, He said, "Walk," and the man walked. To the adulterous woman, He said, "Go and sin no more," and she was set free. To the disciples in the boat on the stormy waves, He said, "Peace, be still," and the wind and waves obeyed! And when He went to the cross to die, His actions said, "I'll take your place."

> *But to all who did receive him,*
> *who believed in his name, he gave the*
> *right to become children of God.*
> JOHN 1:12 ESV

## PERSONAL APPLICATION:

God is working behind the scenes for your good. When your circumstances look grim or it's difficult to see God moving, be assured He's alive and active. Jesus always "lives to make intercession" for those who draw near to God (Hebrews 7:25 ESV). He works on your behalf. When it seems like no one else is in your corner, Jesus "sticks closer than a brother" (Proverbs 18:24 ESV).

When you think of someone who has no one to speak up on his or her behalf, who comes to mind? God calls us to be a voice for the voiceless, first through prayer and then through action. Will you extend Christ's love to the lost, the weak, the helpless, and the alone?

## PRAYER FOR TODAY:

*Dearest Jesus, thank You for loving me and dying for me. I'm so grateful I'm part of Your family. Thank You that You're interceding for me at this very moment. Please be my defender and work on my behalf in this area of my life: [Add the specific area]. Open my eyes and show me how I can help someone who has no voice. In Jesus' name, amen.*

———————— ※ ————————

*"I will be a father to you, and you shall be sons and daughters to me, says the Lord Almighty."*
2 CORINTHIANS 6:18 ESV

# Day 5
# WAITING

*Wait for the Lord; be strong,
and let your heart take courage;
wait for the Lord!*
PSALM 27:14 ESV

> "Pity was suddenly stirring in her heart for the child. What a starved, unloved life she had had—a life of drudgery and poverty and neglect." (CH. 5)

After her first evening at Green Gables with all of its stormy emotions, Anne puts on a brave face as best she can the next day. She seems to sense that tears and dramatic outbursts won't do any good. Despite feeling like her life is a "perfect graveyard of buried hopes," Anne shows a surprising amount of restraint. When it's time to leave Green Gables, she doesn't look back; instead, she sets her "mind firmly" to enjoying the drive.

As they drive to Mrs. Spencer's house, Marilla asks Anne about her past. She says, "I don't want any of your imaginings. Just you stick to bald facts." Anne provides a brief personal history, telling Marilla as succinctly and politely as she can about the women for whom she has worked. However, Marilla is "shrewd enough to read between the lines" and soon realizes the full extent of Anne's "poverty and neglect."

Pity stirs in Marilla's heart as she realizes what a profoundly sad, hard life Anne has lived. Her resolve wavers: "What if she,

Marilla, should indulge Matthew's unaccountable whim and let her stay?" Marilla ponders the question as they continue to drive. Beside her, Anne fixes her eyes on the shore and gives herself up "to a silent rapture" over its beauty.

Anne's resolute waiting is a picture of the stillness that's essential to waiting on God. Anne's controlled demeanor, though she's terribly sad and disappointed, brings to mind the calm that comes after a storm. Though there's wreckage, everything is still. Though the clouds linger, the rain has stopped. In the same way, when we're faced with chaotic and uncertain circumstances, there comes a time when we must cease striving, set our racing thoughts and emotions firmly aside, and wait for God to move: "You will keep in perfect peace all who trust in you, all whose thoughts are fixed on you!" (Isaiah 26:3 NLT).

The Bible says the Lord fights for us when we face insurmountable odds and have no hope of victory. All He asks of us is that we stand still: "The LORD will fight for you; you need only to be still" (Exodus 14:14 NIV). The "LORD Almighty" is with you (Psalm 46:7 NIV), fighting the battles you can't fight. He promises never to leave you nor forsake you (Hebrews 13:5). Though you're caught in the fray, the battle is His.

> *"This is what the LORD says: Do not be afraid!*
> *Don't be discouraged by this mighty army,*
> *for the battle is not yours, but God's."*
> 2 CHRONICLES 20:15 NLT

## PERSONAL APPLICATION:

If you are in a difficult time of waiting, resist the temptation to make things happen in your own strength. Don't try to manipulate people or circumstances. Instead, allow God to do His work in His way. Commit yourself to steadfast daily prayer. Wait on the Lord with firm resolve. Quiet your heart before Him. Choose not to panic, not to fight, not to run, but to wait.

It takes time for hearts to soften, for people to relent, for thoughts to shift, for circumstances to change. Remember this: God is with you in the waiting, moving in ways you can't see, and He has plans and purposes for you *while* you wait. Take a look around—there may be someone in the waiting room with you who could use a prayer partner and friend.

## PRAYER FOR TODAY:

*Lord Jesus, thank You that You are able to touch hearts and change minds. Please soften my heart to Your work and move in the hearts of the people around me. I pray for Your quiet assurance as I wait, especially in regard to the situations I can't control. I come before You now and wait for You to move in this area of my life. [Add your specific request.] In Jesus' name, amen.*

---

*Be still, and know that I am God.*
PSALM 46:10 KJV

# Day 6
# THE GOD WHO SEES

—※—

*When he saw the crowds, he had compassion*
*on them, because they were harassed and*
*helpless, like sheep without a shepherd.*
MATTHEW 9:36 NIV

> " 'Oh, Miss Cuthbert, did you really say that perhaps you would let me stay at Green Gables?' she said, in a breathless whisper, as if speaking aloud might shatter the glorious possibility. 'Did you really say it? Or did I only imagine that you did?' " (CH. 6)

In this chapter, Anne finds herself—once again—at the mercy of others. Whatever the strangers say, whatever the adults decide, that will settle the matter. In this moment, Anne has no voice, no power, and no way out. She needs someone to step in and help her; she needs someone to see, to understand, and to care.

As Anne's future hangs in the balance, Marilla looks across the room. And what she sees changes everything: "Marilla looked at Anne and softened at the sight of the child's pale face with its look of mute misery—the misery of a helpless little creature who finds itself once more caught in the trap from which it had escaped." Her heart softens with compassion and she knows she must say something. If she doesn't, the "helpless little creature" will go to yet another unhappy home with yet another hard and unyielding taskmaster.

Anne needs a lifeline that only Marilla has the power to give. So Marilla intervenes and says she'd better take Anne home and "talk it over with Matthew" first. As Marilla speaks, a "sunrise" dawns on Anne's face: "First the look of despair faded out; then came a faint flush of hope; her eyes grew deep and bright as morning stars. The child was quite transfigured." With just a few words, the trajectory of Anne's whole life is forever altered.

In many ways, this scene mirrors our lives apart from God. Without Him, we're across the room, separated from the love we've always wanted. But Christ sees us sitting across the gap, and His compassion is great. He extends His hands to us in welcome. He speaks and everything changes. Despair fades out, the flush of hope appears, and a new light dawns. With Him, we are indeed "transfigured."

Jesus deeply loves the very people society says are worthless. During His earthly ministry, He fed, healed, and broke bread with the people society rejected—the homeless, the disfigured, the oppressed, the unwanted, and the alone. He came for the lost and the lonely. He looked at people and was moved to compassion because He saw that they were like sheep without a shepherd.

> *Jesus said to them, "It is not the healthy*
> *who need a doctor, but the sick. I have not*
> *come to call the righteous, but sinners."*
> MARK 2:17 NIV

## PERSONAL APPLICATION:

Jesus not only sees us, He came "to seek and to save the lost" (Luke 19:10 ESV). "Jesus Christ is the same yesterday and today and forever" (Hebrews 13:8 ESV). If you don't know Jesus as your personal Savior, He's seeking to save you. Please invite Him into your heart today. If you do know Jesus but you're feeling distant or alone, He's inviting you to come close and rest in His arms.

We all need someone to step in and change the path and pattern of our lives. Ask God to open your eyes to the needs of the people around you. You may see pain hidden behind bravado or tears lurking at the edges of a smile. If you notice someone struggling or in distress, take the time to step across the gap and offer to talk and pray together.

## PRAYER FOR TODAY:

*Dearest Lord, thank You for Your great love and compassion for me. I'm so glad You see me and care for me. When I feel like I'm far from You, I ask you to pull me close. Be my good shepherd. Please speak life into the areas of my heart where I need Your compassion and help most. [Add your prayer request.] In Jesus' name, amen.*

———————✳———————

*[Hagar] gave this name to the LORD who spoke to her: "You are the God who sees me."*
GENESIS 16:13 NIV

## Day 7
# FIRSTS OF FAITH

※

*Do not despise these small beginnings,
for the LORD rejoices to see the work begin.*
ZECHARIAH 4:10 NLT

> "Why must people kneel down to pray? If I really wanted to pray I'll tell you what I'd do. I'd go out into a great big field all alone or into the deep, deep, woods, and I'd look up into the sky—up-up-up—into that lovely blue sky that looks as if there was no end to its blueness. And then I'd just feel a prayer." (CH. 7)

In this bedtime scene, Anne expresses to Marilla her most honest feelings about prayer and faith. She confesses that she never prays and that she doesn't care about God because she was told He made her hair red "on purpose." When Marilla asks Anne if she knows "who God is," Anne recites a memorized catechism.

When it's time to pray, Anne buries her head in Marilla's lap and says the best, most "flowery prayer" she can think up in the moment. Marilla is "only preserved from complete collapse by remembering that it was not irreverence, but simply spiritual ignorance" that led Anne to pray that way. She decides Anne's "religious training" must begin at once.

Though Marilla thinks Anne must be "next door to a perfect heathen," she also realizes something profound: Anne knows "nothing about God's love" because she has "never had it translated to her through the medium of human love." A loving God is just as foreign to Anne as a family who loves and wants her.

Anne knows a little bit *about* God, and her heart is in the right place, but she doesn't yet know or love God.

Many people know something *of* God but don't have a personal, loving relationship *with* Him. Others have difficulty understanding and receiving God's love because they've been hurt by the people who were supposed to love them the most. And religion, when it's merely a set of rules to follow, rarely brings about new life. But love—love changes everything. God loves you more than any person ever could, and He invites you to trust Him with your whole heart. Truly, God so loved *you* that He gave His *only* Son, so that you might believe in Him and "not perish but have eternal life" (John 3:16 ESV).

Your firsts of faith—even your baby steps—are precious in God's sight. Every prayer, whether eloquent or stuttered, is dear to Him. There is great rejoicing "before the angels of God" when someone accepts Christ (Luke 15:10 ESV)! And as you grow in your faith, God encourages and supports your efforts just like a delighted father does with a toddler learning to crawl, then walk, then run.

> *"I have loved you with an everlasting love;*
> *I have drawn you with unfailing kindness."*
> JEREMIAH 31:3 NIV

## PERSONAL APPLICATION:

Anne's ideal place to pray—out in a big field, looking up into the sky, and *feeling* a prayer—is a beautiful expression of worship. Whether we're new to the faith or have known God for years, we all need time to enjoy the fullness of God and bask in His presence. When life gets busy, it's important to make time and space to stop and look up.

Take some time today to find a spot where you can worship and pray without interruption. In the quiet, as you come before God in praise and adoration, you might feel inspired to utter special, consecrated prayers or you may simply want to be still before Him. Ask the Holy Spirit to lead you, speak to you, and refresh your soul.

## PRAYER FOR TODAY:

*Lord Jesus, thank You for taking so much pleasure in my baby steps of faith. Thank You for hearing my prayers and helping me grow. I come before You now in an extended time of worship. Please lead me in new steps of faith and help me to be still before You. [Add your prayer request.] In Jesus' name, amen.*

*And pray in the Spirit on all occasions with all kinds of prayers and requests.*
EPHESIANS 6:18 NIV

# Day 8
# A Forever Home

*Consequently, you are no longer foreigners and strangers, but fellow citizens with God's people and also members of his household.*
Ephesians 2:19 NIV

> "It's a million times nicer to be Anne of Green Gables than Anne of nowhere in particular, isn't it?" (CH. 8)

When Anne discovers the portrait of "Christ Blessing Little Children" in the sitting room at Green Gables, it strikes a chord with her. She identifies with the little girl "standing off by herself in the corner as if she didn't belong to anybody." Anne doesn't have any family or friends. She doesn't remember her parents. She has never had a home or a room of her own.

Anne knows firsthand what it feels like to belong nowhere and to no one. She has never been welcomed or wanted. It's not surprising that Anne wants to call Marilla "Aunt Marilla" or that she longs for a bosom friend, "a really kindred spirit to whom [she] can confide [her] inmost soul." Until now, Anne has experienced a string of harsh, burdensome realities with only her imagination and make-believe friends for comfort.

In this chapter, after an agonizing wait, Anne finds out that Matthew and Marilla have decided to keep her. No one has ever offered to adopt her; she has never been part of a family. She's overwhelmed when Marilla tells her the happy news: " 'I'm crying,' said Anne in a tone of bewilderment. 'I can't think why. I'm glad as glad can be.' " It's the first time any of her dreams has come true.

Like Anne, we all want to belong somewhere, to someone. No one likes to be the one standing off to the side, the one no one notices, the one who doesn't fit in. From young school children to senior citizens, humans yearn to feel included. We join clubs, enroll in classes, and sign up for group projects, book clubs, and outings—all for the sake of togetherness. We love finding our people and our "tribe." We're made for connection and community.

Perhaps your earthly father wasn't loving or kind—maybe you've never had a Matthew Cuthbert in your life. Here's the good news: In Christ, you are no longer so-and-so from nowhere in particular; you are a child of God and a "co-heir with Christ" (Romans 8:17 NIV)! You are no longer a foreigner or a stranger; instead, you are a fellow citizen with God's people and a member of His household (Ephesians 2:19).

*See what kind of love the Father has given to us,*
*that we should be called children of God; and so we are.*
1 JOHN 3:1 ESV

## PERSONAL APPLICATION:

We're all searching for our forever home. There's a reason we long for family, for bosom friends, for a place where we belong. We're built for love and commitment, for family and home. If you feel as though you're standing on the sidelines, like you don't fit in or haven't found your niche, be encouraged: God has a place carved out for you in the body of Christ. Make sure you plug into a local church and join a small group there. We aren't meant to walk this life alone.

Keep your eyes open for people standing on the edges. God invites you to help others feel like they belong. You can welcome people into your world by waving them over, including them in a conversation, or going to greet them. Even a small gesture of kindness can cause a ripple effect in someone's life— one that you may not even realize.

## PRAYER FOR TODAY:

*Lord Jesus, thank You for welcoming me into Your forever family. Thank You that I belong to You! Please help me understand what it truly means to be a child of God. Please show me the place You are calling me to serve at my church. Use me to reach out to people who are on the edges: [add specific names here]. In Jesus' name, amen.*

———————— ✳ ————————

*For since the world began, no ear has heard and no eye has seen a God like you, who works for those who wait for him!*
ISAIAH 64:4 NLT

# Day 9
# OLD SCARS

---

*Therefore, if anyone is in Christ,
he is a new creation. The old has
passed away; behold, the new has come.*
2 CORINTHIANS 5:17 ESV

> " 'Just imagine how you would feel if somebody told you to your face that you were skinny and ugly,' pleaded Anne tearfully." (CH. 9)

Anne says this to Marilla on the heels of a dramatic incident, during which Mrs. Rachel Lynde said harsh and unkind things about Anne's appearance. In response, Anne lost her temper and flew at Mrs. Lynde in a mad rage, screaming at her and stamping her foot. It's clear that Mrs. Lynde's hurtful words hit a nerve with Anne and triggered an emotional outburst rooted in deep pain.

Anne doesn't expect compliments. She knows she's too skinny, her face is freckled, and her hair is "as red as carrots" (ch. 9). But hearing someone else confirm her worst thoughts about herself is more than she can take: " 'Oh, but there's such a difference between saying a thing yourself and hearing other people say it,' wailed Anne. 'You may know a thing is so, but you can't help hoping other people don't quite think it is.' "

When Marilla scolds her about her behavior toward Mrs. Lynde, Anne asks how she would feel if it happened to her. Suddenly, an "old remembrance" comes to Marilla's mind: "She had been a very small child when she had heard one aunt say of her to another, 'What a pity she is such a dark, homely little thing.' Marilla was every day of fifty before the sting had gone out of that memory." Marilla softens and admits that even though Anne shouldn't have lashed out, her feelings are understandable.

Words hurt. We all carry scars from the names we've been called, the labels we've been given, and the things people have said about us. And the more we hear those negative terms, the more it affects the way we act and think. We begin to internalize the things we hear about ourselves, regardless of whether they're true. Unkind names and labels take deep root. We can hear their echo decades later. Names like Ugly. Loser. Skinny. Fat. Unwanted. Dumb. Freckled. Red-haired. Carrots.

But here's the good news: In Christ, you are a new creation. The old has passed away and the new has come (2 Corinthians 5:17)! The day you accepted Jesus as your Savior, He washed you of all your sin and guilt. Everything you were then is now part of your "before Christ" story. Your old names and labels have passed away. Now you have a host of new names. Names like Beloved. Cherished. Redeemed. Restored. Forgiven. Reborn. Free. Loved. Wanted.

*Instead, let the Spirit renew your thoughts and attitudes. Put on your new nature, created to be like God—truly righteous and holy.*
EPHESIANS 4:23-24 NLT

## Personal Application:

We all carry around old scars. And we each have at least one Rachel Lynde in our lives. Whether on purpose or not, their words always seem to carry a barb. Their taunts cause us to lose our cool, lash out, or respond in anger. But while we can't control how people talk to us or treat us, we can decide how we respond.

In Christ we are set free from slavery to sin and set free to choose new behaviors and reactions. The more we listen to what Jesus says about us, the less we care about what people say or think. And remember, hurting people often hurt other people. That person who jabs at you probably carries scars too. Either way, take time to pray and prepare your heart before the next time you see him or her.

## Prayer for Today:

*Dearest Lord, thank You for giving me a new name and identity. Please help me stand in my identity as Your child, so that I can respond graciously to others and find my confidence in You alone. I lift up to You the old scars and labels I carry, and I ask for Your healing touch. [Add your prayer request.] In Jesus' name, amen.*

---

*Therefore, as God's chosen people, holy and dearly loved, clothe yourselves with compassion, kindness, humility, gentleness and patience.*
Colossians 3:12 niv

# Day 10
# PURSUING PEACE

*If it is possible, as far as it depends on you,*
*live at peace with everyone.*
ROMANS 12:18 NIV

> "I have no hard feelings against Mrs. Lynde now. It gives you a lovely, comfortable feeling to apologize and be forgiven, doesn't it?" (CH. 10)

This touching moment occurs as Anne and Marilla walk home from Mrs. Lynde's house after Anne's apology. During the days prior, Green Gables is in a state of upset: "Breakfast, dinner, and supper were very silent meals." Anne stubbornly refuses to apologize to Mrs. Lynde for the things she said, so Marilla puts her foot down and won't let Anne leave her room until she does. Gentle Matthew is caught in the middle: he asks Marilla not to be "too hard on her" and checks Anne's untouched food trays with a "troubled eye."

Matthew is the one who finally brokers peace. He sneaks up to the east gable and asks Anne to apologize. His loving and quiet appeal prompts an immediate response. Anne admits she was wrong and says she feels "ashamed" of herself now that her anger has burned itself out. She says, "It would be true enough to say I am sorry, because I *am* sorry now." Only her fear of humiliation holds her back from doing what's right. Matthew's gentle encouragement helps do the rest, and Anne agrees to go.

After Anne's rather dramatic apology, peace comes again. Anne and Mrs. Lynde are on good terms; Anne and Marilla are back in step; and Matthew can look forward to a happier, more companionable kitchen table. As they walk home toward the "cheerful light" of the kitchen at Green Gables, Anne slips her hand into Marilla's in a moment of sweet communion: "Something warm and pleasant welled up in Marilla's heart at the touch of that thin little hand in her own—a throb of the maternity she had missed, perhaps."

Apologies and forgiveness do give us "a lovely, comfortable feeling." Repentance and restoration bring enormous relief. These precious acts of humility close the gap between us and God and between us and other people. Romans 12:18 (NIV) says, "If it is possible, as far as it depends on you, live at peace with everyone." That means that you and I need to do everything we can to live at peace with others—it means we're not easily offended, we're quick to ask for forgiveness, and we don't stir up trouble.

As Christ's followers, we're called to be peacemakers and grace givers. God asks us to be the first to make things right. Sometimes that means asking someone to forgive you. Other times it means forgiving others just as God forgave us.

*Be kind and compassionate to one another,*
*forgiving each other, just as in Christ God forgave you.*
EPHESIANS 4:32 NIV

# PERSONAL APPLICATION:

Have you been hurt? Or have you perhaps done the hurting? Making peace is the brave thing to do. Asking for forgiveness or extending forgiveness is a big first step. Even though it's difficult, opening a wound, gently cleaning it out, and bandaging it is a Jesus action. It might be painful or awkward, but we honor the Lord when we humble ourselves and "seek peace and pursue it" (Psalm 34:14; 1 Peter 3:11 NIV).

We are accountable for our own actions and speech. As Christ's representatives, it's important to be above reproach as much as possible. No one acts perfectly all the time. We lash out. We say things we regret. But it's what we do with our mistakes that counts. When you say or do something that's hurtful, make it right with the Lord and the other person right away.

# PRAYER FOR TODAY:

*Lord Jesus, I confess to You the times I've been harsh or unkind, impatient or unloving. I want to be right with You and treat others with kindness. Please forgive my sins and give me Your heart of love. I lift to You now the unforgiveness I carry toward others. [Add any specific instances.] Please bring healing and restoration. In Jesus' name, amen.*

---

*"Repent, then, and turn to God, so that your sins may be wiped out, that times of refreshing may come from the Lord."*
ACTS 3:19 NIV

# Day 11
# THE SECRET PLACE

*"But when you pray, go into your room and shut the door and pray to your Father who is in secret. And your Father who sees in secret will reward you."*
MATTHEW 6:6 ESV

> "[Mr. Bell] was talking to God and he didn't seem to be very much interested in it, either. I think he thought God was too far away to make it worth while. I said a little prayer myself, though. . . . I just said, 'Thank you for it, God,' two or three times." (CH. 11)

In this chapter, Anne attends church for the first time. She arrives in a stiff black-and-white sateen dress and a new hat, which she has "liberally garlanded" with buttercups and wild roses. The other girls stare at her "extraordinary head adornment" and whisper to each other "behind their quarterlies." No one makes any "friendly advances," but Anne manages to find her way around and keep herself entertained.

Anne's report to Marilla upon returning home is humorous: she describes Mr. Bell's "awfully long prayer," the Sunday school teacher who asked a lot of questions (but wouldn't answer any), and the minister's sermon that wasn't a "bit interesting." Marilla wants to scold Anne for her criticism and wandering thoughts, but she's hampered by "the undeniable fact that some of the things" Anne said were what "she herself had really thought deep down in her heart for years." Anne's honest point of view brings to light an important truth: the people at Marilla's church don't seem very enthusiastic about their faith.

The bright spot in Anne's morning at church is her own personal communion with God as she sits and looks out the window during the sermon. The simple prayer she prays in the quiet of her heart is a natural outpouring of thanks as she admires the "long row of white birches hanging over the lake" and considers her new life at Green Gables.

While Mr. Bell seems to think God is "too far off," Anne instinctively knows God is near. Her prayer reminds us that we can draw near to God and enjoy His presence at any time and in any place. We can speak to Him in the quiet of our hearts and invite Him into our thoughts, our dreams, and our worries. Our prayers don't need to be long or elaborate. Simple prayers uttered throughout the day cultivate a wonderful sense of personal fellowship with God.

Daily devotions help us focus on God, seek His guidance, study His Word, and give Him thanks. In the Bible, Jacob got up early to pour out an offering to God (Genesis 28:18); Daniel prayed on his knees three times each day (Daniel 6:10); Hannah got up from eating and poured out her heart to God for a child (1 Samuel 1:15–16); and King David woke early to praise God (Psalm 57:8). Jesus Himself often withdrew to pray in the quiet morning hours.

> *Very early in the morning, while it was*
> *still dark, Jesus got up, left the house and*
> *went off to a solitary place, where he prayed.*
> MARK 1:35 NIV

## PERSONAL APPLICATION:

Daily devotions are a precious gift from the Lord. That quiet, secret place in your heart—the place where you meet with God—is a place that's for you and Him alone. It's your communion place. It's where you can retreat from everything else and find peace. In the stillness, He is there.

Jesus is inviting you to come away with Him today. Take time to slow down and be still before the Lord. Turn everything off; put everything away. Find a quiet place, whether it's your closet or car or bedroom or garden. Sit before Him, eyes closed, and breathe. Raise your hands to Him in adoration. Invite the Holy Spirit to fall afresh on you and breathe new life into your soul.

## PRAYER FOR TODAY:

*Thank You, Jesus, for reminding me to come away with You. You are my peace, my hiding place, my shelter, and my refuge. Please help me set aside everything else and devote this time to You. I ask You to please quiet my heart and speak life to me. I lay down all my burdens at Your feet. [Add your prayer request.] In Jesus' name, amen.*

---

*Whoever dwells in the shelter of the Most High will rest in the shadow of the Almighty.*
PSALM 91:1 NIV

# Day 12
# BOSOM FRIENDS

———————— ✳ ————————

*A friend loves at all times.*
PROVERBS 17:17 ESV

> " 'Oh, Diana,' said Anne at last, clasping her hands and speaking almost in a whisper, 'oh, do you think you can like me a little—enough to be my bosom friend?' " (CH. 12)

When Anne and Diana finally meet, Anne is excited, nervous, and worried. She isn't sure Diana will like her, but Marilla warns her that Diana's mother is the one to worry about: "If she has heard about your outburst to Mrs. Lynde and going to church with buttercups round your hat, I don't know what she'll think of you. You must be polite and well behaved, and don't make any of your startling speeches."

Anne arrives trembling at the Barry house and manages to keep from saying anything too strange. When she sees Diana for the first time, Diana is sitting and reading a book: "She was a very pretty little girl, with her mother's black eyes and hair, and rosy cheeks, and the merry expression which was her inheritance from her father." Diana is good-natured and fun. She's quick to laugh and finds Anne entertaining.

Out in the garden—with her signature intensity—Anne abruptly asks Diana to be her bosom friend. Diana laughs, saying it'll be "jolly" to have a girl to play with. Anne suggests they make a solemn promise to be faithful friends "as long as the sun and moon shall endure." Diana repeats the oath "with a laugh fore and aft." And with that vow, Anne's lifelong dream of a bosom friend finally comes true. Diana becomes Anne's devoted best friend, confidante, and supporter from that moment on.

We all long for a bosom friend, an "intimate friend," a true "kindred spirit" with whom we can share our "inmost soul" (ch. 8). Friendship, fellowship, and community are an integral part of God's design. We're built for committed, loving relationships. Jesus calls us His friends (John 15:15) and promises to be with us to the "end of the age" (Matthew 28:20 NASB). He also invites us to become active participants of the body of Christ in a local church (Romans 12:5) so that we can grow in our faith and encourage one another (Hebrews 10:24–25).

In the Bible, Ruth pledged to stay with her mother-in-law, Naomi, even though it meant leaving her family and home. Ruth said, "Do not urge me to leave you or to return from following you. For where you go I will go, and where you lodge I will lodge. Your people shall be my people, and your God my God" (Ruth 1:16 ESV). Ruth refused to be separated from Naomi and remained by her side as they forged a new life in Israel.

*"I will never leave you nor forsake you."*
HEBREWS 13:5 ESV

## PERSONAL APPLICATION:

Do you long for a bosom friend? There are kindred spirits out there who need your friendship too! Even though Anne perhaps felt more desperate, Diana also needed a friend. You need people in your life who will stand with you and walk beside you through thick and thin. If you're in search of a few faithful friends, start with daily prayer and regular church attendance. Ask God to open your eyes and help you make connections with like-hearted people.

If you open your heart and let God choose your friends and companions, His selection often provides a sweet surprise. He likes to fit us together with people who balance us. God loves variety in all of creation—in the pattern of a butterfly's wings, in the texture of a person's hair, in the shape of the clouds in the sky—and in relationships. We don't need people exactly like us; we need people who understand us, encourage us, and challenge us.

## PRAYER FOR TODAY:

*Lord Jesus, thank You for being my lifelong bosom friend. I'm so glad You're always with me wherever I go, through every season of life. I ask You now to deepen my friendships. Please draw me close to committed, caring, and godly friends. Show me how to be a better friend to the following people: [Add names]. In Jesus' name, amen.*

---

*"Greater love has no one than this, that someone lay down his life for his friends."*
JOHN 15:13 ESV

# Day 13
# STARTLING SWEETNESS

---※---

*"Give, and it will be given to you. A good measure, pressed down, shaken together and running over, will be poured into your lap."*
LUKE 6:38 NIV

> "Anne cast herself into Marilla's arms and rapturously kissed her sallow cheek. It was the first time in her whole life that childish lips had voluntarily touched Marilla's face. Again that sudden sensation of startling sweetness thrilled her." (CH. 13)

In this scene, Marilla agrees to allow Anne to attend the Sunday school picnic. Anne is overwhelmed by so much goodness. She has never been to a picnic, never had ice cream, and never experienced the things other girls her age enjoy regularly. In her excitement, she hugs and kisses Marilla, a gesture Marilla has never experienced before. Marilla says Anne needs to "sober down a little and learn to be steady," yet she's "secretly vastly pleased at Anne's impulsive caress."

Marilla is continually surprised by Anne's love and affection. Her way of thinking and doing things is completely foreign to Marilla. While Marilla is cautious, practical, and subdued, Anne is "rapturous," "impulsive," and "poetical." When Marilla worries that Anne is getting her hopes up, Anne relishes the "delights of anticipation." Though Marilla tells Anne that she sets her "heart too much on things," Anne says that "looking forward to things is half the pleasure of them."

Marilla's whole world is changing, and she's experiencing things she never imagined. She took a brave step of faith in adopting Anne, thinking it was her Christian duty, but her eyes are opening to all that it means to be a mother. Marilla predicted a lot of hard work and difficulty in bringing up Anne, but there was one thing she didn't anticipate: joy. Walls are coming down; love is springing up. Unexpected blessings are now being poured into her lap.

When we give of ourselves in an effort to love and serve God, we receive eternal gifts of startling sweetness in return. The beauty of God's economy is astounding. When we give, we receive. When we seek to bless, we are blessed in return. And when we pour out the best of our time, efforts, and gifts, God works in ways we can't imagine.

When Ruth left her family to stay by Naomi's side, God gave her a husband, a son, and a place in the family of God (Ruth 4). When Hannah gave her young son Samuel to serve in the temple, God blessed her with three more sons and two daughters (1 Samuel 2). And when the widow offered Elijah the last of her flour and oil, God provided enough flour and oil for her and her son through the end of the famine (1 Kings 17). In each case, the sweet harvest moments came after long periods of sacrifice and waiting.

*Whoever sows bountifully will also reap bountifully.*
2 CORINTHIANS 9:6 ESV

## PERSONAL APPLICATION:

Are you worn out with waiting for the harvest? Do you feel as though your efforts are in vain, that fruit is nonexistent or long in coming? In some of our endeavors, we see obvious growth, quick outcomes, and visible fruit from our labors. But there are many seasons of life—such as school, marriage, parenting, ministry, and work—that require extended long-term efforts.

More often the reality of ministry, service, and loving others requires great quantities of faith and patience. It's tempting to think you're not making a difference, but don't become discouraged. God is working in ways you can't imagine. Keep your eyes open for moments of startling sweetness. And remember, even if you don't see fruit here on earth, you're laying up treasure in heaven!

## PRAYER FOR TODAY:

*Lord, Jesus, I confess to You my discouragement.*
*When I don't see clear results, I sometimes lose heart.*
*I want to serve You and please You in every good work.*
*Please help me notice and encourage the efforts of others*
*around me. I need Your reassurance in this area of my life:*
*[name the specific area]. In Jesus' name, amen.*

---

*Let us not become weary in doing good,*
*for at the proper time we will reap*
*a harvest if we do not give up.*
GALATIANS 6:9 NIV

# *Day 14*
# WALKING THROUGH FIRE

---※---

*"When you pass through the waters, I will be with you;
and when you pass through the rivers, they will not
sweep over you. When you walk through the fire, you
will not be burned; the flames will not set you ablaze."*
ISAIAH 43:2 NIV

> " 'I believe you are telling me a falsehood, Anne,' [Marilla] said sharply." (CH. 14)

In this chapter, Anne is falsely accused of something she didn't do. When Marilla's amethyst brooch goes missing, she's convinced Anne took it and lost it. She says Anne can't leave her room or attend the picnic until she confesses. But when Anne makes up a fake confession, it only makes things worse. Marilla tells Matthew, "It's a dreadful thing to think she tells falsehoods. It's a far worse thing than her fit of temper. It's a fearful responsibility to have a child in your house you can't trust. Slyness and untruthfulness—that's what she has displayed."

The resulting storm that blows through Green Gables disturbs everyone in the house. Anne, "tear-stained" and tragic, is stuck in her room. Marilla feels upset and "deserted by everyone." Even Matthew feels "forlorn" and caught in the middle: he can't "so quickly lose faith" in Anne, but he admits that the circumstances "are against her." Meals downstairs without Anne are "dismal."

This situation isn't just about a brooch—it's about trust. No matter what Anne says, Marilla refuses to believe the truth. And unfortunately, Anne's false confession only serves to confirm Marilla's opinion of her. If things had gone differently and Marilla hadn't found the brooch and apologized to Anne, this situation could have become a source of doubt and mistrust for years to come. The truth eventually sets Anne free, but she has to walk through fire first.

Friction in relationships is one of the hardest battles we fight as Christians. Even small misunderstandings, when they aren't dealt with in grace and humility, can create giant fissures. But when trust is at stake, it's especially difficult. When we've been wronged, we need to draw close to God more than ever and ask Him to purify our hearts and restore our spirits so that we don't become hardened or bitter.

Many of God's followers faced unjust accusations, angry people, and messy situations. Joseph was put in prison for a crime he didn't commit (Genesis 39). Daniel was thrown in the lions' den for praying (Daniel 6). Stephen was killed for testifying about Jesus (Acts 7). And Paul and Silas were severely beaten and thrown into jail for preaching the Gospel (Acts 16). When we are in the thick of it, God walks with us through the fire and the flood (Isaiah 43:2).

> *For in the day of trouble he will keep me safe*
> *in his dwelling; he will hide me in the shelter*
> *of his sacred tent and set me high upon a rock.*
>
> PSALM 27:5 NIV

## PERSONAL APPLICATION:

Are you in the midst of a misunderstanding or disagreement with someone? Have you been accused of something you didn't do? Does everything you say seem to make it worse? So much pain is involved when relationships are torn up and people are at odds, especially when there's a long or drawn out conflict.

This is your immediate call to faithful and determined prayer. The only one who can soften hearts and change attitudes is God. Begin by praying for an open, responsive heart. Humbly ask the Lord to search your heart and show you anything that's amiss. Then ask God to soften the heart of the other person. If you need truth to come to light, harmony restored, and ice to melt, you need time on your knees.

## PRAYER FOR TODAY:

*Lord, thank You that You understand the details of my situation. I ask You to first soften my heart and give me new eyes to see. I need Your help to make things right and bring restoration. Please mend hearts and bring compassion, harmony, and unity back in this area of my life: [Name the specific area]. In Jesus' name, amen.*

---

*Create in me a clean heart, O God,
and renew a right spirit within me.*
PSALM 51:10 ESV

# Day 15
# CRACKED SLATES

*Be angry and do not sin; do not
let the sun go down on your anger,
and give no opportunity to the devil.*
Ephesians 4:26-27 esv

> " 'I shall never forgive Gilbert Blythe,'
> said Anne firmly. 'And Mr. Phillips
> spelled my name without an e too. The iron
> has entered into my soul, Diana.' " (CH. 15)

School starts off well for Anne, but trouble brews when Gilbert Blythe returns to school. First, he winks at her. Then, because he isn't "used to putting himself out to make a girl look at him," he picks up her braid and calls her by the dreaded name "Carrots." In a fit of anger, Anne breaks her slate over his head and is punished by Mr. Phillips in front of the whole class.

From there, things go from bad to worse. When a group of students arrives late to class after lunch the next day, Mr. Phillips makes Anne the "scapegoat." For Anne, it's the "end of all things." It's bad enough to be "singled out for punishment from among a dozen equally guilty" students and "worse still" to have to sit by a boy. But it heaps "insult on injury to a degree utterly unbearable" that the boy is Gilbert. Anne puts her head on her desk and seethes "with shame and anger and humiliation."

Gilbert says he's "awfully sorry" and tries to make amends with a "little pink candy heart," but Anne refuses to forgive him and crushes the heart under her heel. She says she won't go back to Mr. Phillips's school and packs up her desk. It takes months before she finally goes back to school and years before she finally forgives Gilbert. The "iron" enters her soul, and her heart hardens into a stubborn rock that won't budge.

We can all relate to Anne's anger and humiliation. It's awful to be singled out, teased, and treated unfairly. When everything seems to be against you, when people hurt or misunderstand you, when there's injustice afoot, it can feel like too much to bear. At times we need to press the Pause button and step back a bit from certain people or situations. However, it's also very important that we don't allow our hurt hearts to become hard hearts.

If anyone in the Old Testament had a reason to be angry, it was Joseph. When he was sold into slavery by his brothers and later put into prison for a crime he didn't commit, he could have become a raging, bitter man. He suffered terrible injustices and lost years of his life in confinement. However, though he experienced deep anguish of heart, he continued to serve God faithfully in each situation. He even forgave his brothers for the terrible thing they did to him.

*Good sense makes one slow to anger,*
*and it is his glory to overlook an offense.*
Proverbs 19:11 esv

## PERSONAL APPLICATION:

Have you allowed a bruised soul to turn into a hardened heart? It's easy to do. However, short-term pain can cause long-term harm if we don't work through it in a healthy way. Anne misses out on Gilbert's friendship for five years—all as a result of her unyielding, unforgiving attitude. When we hold on to hurt feelings, we lock ourselves in a prison and miss out on the people and possibilities around us.

Don't get stuck in a rut. Don't let the enemy get a foothold. It's time to move forward with God's help. If you need to let go of past hurt or need encouragement in a difficult situation, spend time reading Joseph's account in Genesis (Genesis 37–50). Let his story reassure you of God's care for you and inspire you to move past pain to forgiveness.

## PRAYER FOR TODAY:

*Dear Lord, thank You for reminding me that holding on to pain only causes more pain. Please help me process personal offenses in a healthy way. Show me someone I can reach out to for prayer and godly wisdom. I ask for Your help to navigate this difficult situation. [Add your specific request.] In Jesus' name, amen.*

---

*Everyone should be quick to listen, slow to speak and slow to become angry, because human anger does not produce the righteousness that God desires.*
JAMES 1:19-20 NIV

# Day 16
# A Tumblerful
# of Trouble

※

*We are hard pressed on every side, but not
crushed; perplexed, but not in despair; persecuted,
but not abandoned; struck down, but not destroyed.*
2 Corinthians 4:8–9 niv

> " 'I must cry,' said Anne. 'My heart is broken. The stars in their courses fight against me, Marilla. Diana and I are parted forever. Oh, Marilla, I little dreamed of this when first we swore our vows of friendship.' " (CH. 16)

This chapter opens with Anne at the height of happiness. She glories in the ecstasies of Green Gables in October with its birches "turned as golden as sunshine," its maples in "royal crimson," and its wild cherry trees in "loveliest shades of dark red and bronzy green." Her beauty-loving soul revels "in the world of color about her." She exclaims to Marilla, "I'm so glad I live in a world where there are Octobers." The pinnacle of her delight is when Marilla says she may invite Diana over for tea while she attends an Aid Society meeting.

And yet, when she least expects it, Anne finds herself plunged into her worst trial yet. During the girls' teatime, Anne unknowingly gives Diana currant wine to drink instead of raspberry cordial. The next day she discovers that Mrs. Barry believes she "set Diana drunk" on purpose. Mrs. Barry, unmoved by Marilla's explanation or Anne's tears of contrition, coldly tells Anne, "I don't think you are a fit little girl for Diana to associate with.

You'd better go home and behave yourself."

In this chapter, Anne is wronged and hurt once again. When Marilla thought Anne lost her brooch, Anne was threatened with the loss of material comforts like picnics and ice cream, but now her friendship with Diana is at stake. From this point on, Anne is no longer allowed to see or talk to Diana. Anne tells Marilla there's "nothing more to do except to pray." That night, utterly without hope, she cries herself to sleep.

When it feels like everything and everyone is against you, remember that there are invisible powers in the heavenly realms fighting *for* you. In every earthly battle, there is an unseen spiritual battle at work—a clash in the spiritual realm. When you are up against a host of troubles, when the enemy launches a full-blown attack, God is at work.

When there's nothing left to do "but pray," that's when God does things we could never imagine. When Deborah was judge over Israel, the Israelites faced off against the Canaanite army—an army so formidable that the Israelite commander refused to go into battle without Deborah! During the battle, however, God used a fascinating array of people and circumstances to save the Israelites (Judges 5): the stars fought "from their courses" (v. 20 ESV), the Kishon River swept away enemy soldiers (v. 21), and a woman killed the Canaanite commander with a tent peg (v. 26).

> *"You shall not fear them, for it is the*
> *LORD your God who fights for you."*
> DEUTERONOMY 3:22 ESV

## PERSONAL APPLICATION:

Whatever battle you find yourself in today, be assured that God is with you: "The LORD will go before you, and the God of Israel will be your rear guard" (Isaiah 52:12 ESV). He surrounds you with songs of deliverance (Psalm 32:7). And Jesus is "interceding" for you at the "right hand of God" (Romans 8:34 NIV).

God is alive and active in your situation. Though it may take time, and though it may happen in an unexpected way, He *will* win the day. The "surpassing greatness of His power toward us who believe" is at work in your life (Ephesians 1:19 NASB). Rest in the knowledge that He is greater than your deepest trials and your fiercest foes.

## PRAYER FOR TODAY:

*Almighty God, I come to You today and ask for Your help in the battle I'm facing. Sometimes it becomes fierce and overwhelming. Only You are strong enough to bring me through to victory. Please take over and fight on my behalf. I invite You to step in and take charge of this situation. [Add your prayer request.] In Jesus' name, amen.*

---

*Some nations boast of their chariots and horses, but we boast in the name of the LORD our God.*
PSALM 20:7 NLT

# Day 17
# STREAMS IN THE DESERT

*I will open rivers on the bare heights, and fountains in the midst of the valleys. I will make the wilderness a pool of water, and the dry land springs of water.*
ISAIAH 41:18 ESV

> "I thought you liked me of course but I never hoped you loved me. Why, Diana, I didn't think anybody could love me. Nobody ever has loved me since I can remember." (CH. 17)

In this chapter, Anne finds herself alone more than ever. She hasn't been attending school on account of Gilbert teasing her and Mr. Phillips punishing her unfairly, and now she's no longer allowed to play with Diana in the "chilly purple autumn twilights." But in the midst of Anne's trial, several important things happen: she goes back to school, learns that her fellow students have missed her, and finds new interest in her studies.

One surprising gift during this time is that Anne finds out that Diana loves her, which provides "a ray of light" in the darkness. She decides to go back to school, because, as she says, "That is all there is left in life for me, now that my friend has been ruthlessly torn from me. In school I can look at her and muse over days departed." To her surprise, returning to school has other bright spots as well. She is "welcomed back to school with open arms" by her peers.

The streams in Anne's desert prove sweet. The girls say her

imagination has "been sorely missed in games, her voice in the singing and her dramatic ability in the perusal aloud of books at dinner hour." She receives blue plums, a yellow pansy cut from a catalog, a "perfectly elegant" new pattern for knit lace, a perfume bottle, and a pretty poem on "pale pink paper scalloped on the edges." And the best gift of all: a secret handwritten note and a new bookmark "out of red tissue paper" from Diana.

When you're in a valley or going through a painful trial, that's often when God sends the most surprising gifts. If you're not careful, you might miss them, but if you keep your eyes open, you'll find reminders of God's love all around you. And if you ask God to encourage your heart, He'll provide sweet springs of water to help raise your spirits.

In times of loss and heartache, God provides spiritual balms and practical, tangible comforts. When we cry out to Him, He brings us into "a spacious place" (Psalm 118:5 NIV). He makes pools in our wilderness seasons and streams in our desert places (Isaiah 41:18). When we're battle-worn and weary, He cares for our wounds and ministers to our hearts. He heals us. He lifts us up. He opens new doors and does things that couldn't happen otherwise.

> *A bruised reed he will not break, and a*
> *smoldering wick he will not snuff out.*
> ISAIAH 42:3 NIV

## PERSONAL APPLICATION:

When you are struggling, God's grace and mercy abound. When you can't take another step, that's when Jesus picks you up. God wants to carry your burdens: "Cast your cares on the LORD and he will sustain you" (Psalm 55:22 NIV). Your problems aren't too heavy or too numerous for God. You can't overwhelm Him; His hands are big enough.

With God there is always hope. There is always a ray of light. If you feel as though you can't go on or that your circumstances are far too difficult, remember this: "Though they stumble, they will never fall, for the LORD holds them by the hand" (Psalm 37:24 NLT). Ask Jesus to encourage your heart today, and watch for the gifts He'll send.

## PRAYER FOR TODAY:

*Lord Jesus, I feel tired and weary. I need a special measure of Your grace and mercy today. Please encourage my heart with small reminders of Your love. Show me how to support others who are weary. I ask You to make streams in the desert areas of my life. [Add your prayer request.] In Jesus' name, amen.*

---

*"Blessed is the one who trusts in the LORD, whose confidence is in him. They will be like a tree planted by the water that sends out its roots by the stream. It does not fear when heat comes; its leaves are always green. It has no worries in a year of drought and never fails to bear fruit."*
JEREMIAH 17:7–8 NIV

# Day 18

# FOR SUCH A TIME AS THIS

———※———

*We know that for those who love God all things work together for good, for those who are called according to his purpose.*
ROMANS 8:28 ESV

> "All things great are wound up with all things little. At first glance it might not seem that the decision of a certain Canadian Premier to include Prince Edward Island in a political tour could have much or anything to do with the fortunes of little Anne Shirley at Green Gables. But it had." (CH. 18)

In this chapter, all things work together for good—for Anne, Diana, and the Barry family. One winter evening when her parents are away, Diana races to Green Gables for help. Her sister, Minnie May, is sick with croup, and the babysitter doesn't know what to do. Matthew rushes to find a doctor while Anne, grabbing a bottle of ipecac, follows Diana. At the Barry home, Anne sets to work "with skill and promptness."

Due to her experience with Mrs. Hammond's three sets of croupy twins, Anne is able to save Minnie May's life. When Matthew finally arrives with the doctor at 3:00 a.m., Minnie May is sleeping soundly. Anne tells the doctor, "I was awfully near giving up in despair. . . . I actually thought she was going to choke to death." She says she gave every drop of the medicine, but she knew it was the "last lingering hope" and a "vain one."

The doctor later explains the severity of the situation to Mr. and Mrs. Barry and marvels at Anne's skill and presence of mind: "I tell you she saved that baby's life, for it would have been too late by the time I got there." He says she's as "smart as they make 'em." It's clear that few adults, let alone a child, would have known what to do. Mrs. Barry apologizes to Anne, thanks her with tears, and welcomes her back into their home. And at last Anne and Diana are reunited.

At the height of the crisis, we read this: "Anne had not brought up three pairs of twins *for nothing*" (emphasis added). The same is true for you. God has fitted you perfectly for your current situation. Your life and experiences have purpose; they're not for nothing. You are the only one who can do what you do in the way you do it. God is at work in your life right now for your good and the good of others. He can redeem the hardest, most painful parts of your life.

In the Old Testament account, when Esther was taken to the king's palace, she had no say in the matter and was cut off from her family and friends. It must have been a sad and frightening time for her. But God was working behind the scenes. She became queen and gained a position of influence. Later, when the Israelites faced annihilation, her cousin Mordecai sent this message to her: "Who knows but that you have come to your royal position for such a time as this?" (Esther 4:14 NIV). After fasting for three days, Esther bravely approached the king and helped spare her people.

*Be strong and take heart,*
*all you who hope in the LORD.*
PSALM 31:24 NIV

## PERSONAL APPLICATION:

Are there circumstances in your life that you don't think could ever work together for good? In the midst of defeat, despair, and discouragement, it is hard to see how things could ever turn out well. But God can redeem even the most hopeless situations. In fact, He is at work—right now—for your good.

God also wants to work through you in the lives of others. He has divine appointments in mind for you. He wants you to minister comfort to others in their time of need. When He calls your name, be ready to move. Pray today for what God wants to do tomorrow. Ask Him to take your present brokenness and make it into future effectiveness.

## PRAYER FOR TODAY:

*Father in heaven, I thank You that You see the beginning from the end. You see my impossible situations and my past failures. Please work all things for good in my life and help me press on in faith. Use me for such a time as this in my daily life. Please prepare me and use me to meet the needs of others. [Add your prayer request.] In Jesus' name, amen.*

---

*Let us hold unswervingly to the hope
we profess, for he who promised is faithful.*
HEBREWS 10:23 NIV

## Day 19
# FACING LIONS

---

*"Be strong and of good courage; do not
be afraid, nor be dismayed, for the LORD
your God is with you wherever you go."*
JOSHUA 1:9 NKJV

> "Kindred spirits are not so scarce as I used to think. It's splendid to find out there are so many of them in the world." (CH. 19)

In this chapter, Anne finds a kindred spirit in an unlikely place. As Anne and Diana prepare for bed at Diana's house after a concert, Anne suggests they race to the spare room bed. Unfortunately, when they land on the bed, they discover that Diana's wealthy great-aunt, Miss Josephine Barry, is already sleeping in it. Anne finds herself in yet another trial, facing yet another angry person.

But Anne is growing up. When she finds out that Miss Barry plans to cut her trip short and withdraw her offer to pay for Diana's music lessons, Anne faces the matter head-on. Right then and there, she decides to beard "the lion in its den" and speak to Miss Barry. Diana says "she'll eat you alive," but Anne walks "resolutely up to the sitting-room door and knock[s]."

Anne's bravery is inspiring. She admits she would "rather walk up to a cannon's mouth" than go in, but she says she has "got to do it." Anne is not one to shrink back from an unpleasant task. She wants to make things right, and she has learned that it's best to face problems directly. The happy result is that Miss Barry forgives Anne, reinstates Diana's music lessons, and becomes Anne's loyal friend and ally.

Circumstances don't always turn out the way we expect; sometimes they turn out better! Regardless of the result, we honor God when we deal with issues proactively. God accepts a "broken and contrite heart" (Psalm 51:17 ESV) and promises to strengthen us when we face intimidating personalities or situations: "The people who know their God shall be strong, and carry out great exploits" (Daniel 11:32 NKJV).

In Daniel 6 Daniel faced a literal lions' den. King Darius's advisers persuaded him to make a law that said no one could worship anyone but the king for thirty days. Then the men watched Daniel and found him praying with his window open and his face toward Jerusalem, just as he always did. He was thrown into a den of hungry lions, but God closed the lions' mouths and kept Daniel safe. As a result of Daniel's brave faith, King Darius gave glory to God and told his entire kingdom to worship the one true God (Daniel 6:25–27)!

*Fear not, for I am with you; be not dismayed, for I am your God; I will strengthen you, I will help you, I will uphold you with my righteous right hand.*
ISAIAH 41:10 ESV

## PERSONAL APPLICATION:

Is God asking you to do something brave? Perhaps you need to smooth out a relationship, correct a misunderstanding, or request something of a person in authority. Do not forget that kindred spirits "are not so scarce" as you might think. Sometimes even the sternest people will soften when approached the right way. The way we relate to others makes a big difference: "A gentle answer deflects anger" (Proverbs 15:1 NLT).

It's important to take extended time to pray before rushing into a situation or conflict. First, ask God to cleanse and purify your heart. Next, ask Him to provide the right timing and the right words to speak. (And wait until He does.) Then, even if it feels like you're walking into a lions' den, walk in bravely, trusting that God is with you.

## PRAYER FOR TODAY:

*Lord Jesus, thank You for reminding me that facing things is better than avoidance. I believe You are calling me to take a step of faith. Please prepare my heart and show me each next step. Infuse me with courage and kindness. I lift up to You my specific situation and ask for Your help and guidance. [Add your prayer request.] In Jesus' name, amen.*

---

*When Daniel was lifted from the [lions'] den, no wound was found on him, because he had trusted in his God.*
DANIEL 6:23 NIV

# Day 20
# LIVING SAVED

※

*The godly will flourish like palm trees and grow strong like the cedars of Lebanon. For they are transplanted to the LORD's own house. They flourish in the courts of our God.*
PSALM 92:12-13 NLT

> "I've been here for a year and
> I've been so happy." (CH. 20)

In a chapter all about a "good imagination gone wrong," Montgomery tells a story within a story. It's the story of the difference a year can make. It's about the changes that have occurred in Anne's life since her adoption. And it's a picture of the radical difference between life as an orphan and life as an adopted daughter. Anne is no longer Anne of nowhere in particular; she is now Anne of Green Gables.

Anne tells Marilla it's a special anniversary: "Oh, Marilla, it was the day I came to Green Gables. I shall never forget it. It was the turning point in my life." Marilla says simply that she is not sorry she adopted Anne, but the narrator shares her deeper feelings: Marilla "wondered how she could have lived before Anne came to Green Gables." Neither of them is the same.

Anne now lives like she belongs. Even the changes in Anne's room are symbolic of the inner changes that have occurred since her adoption: "In all essential respects the little gable chamber was unchanged. The walls were as white, the pincushion as hard, the chairs as stiffly and yellowly upright as ever. Yet the whole character of the room was altered." We learn that the room is now "full of a new vital, pulsing personality that seemed to pervade it." It's filled with "splendid filmy tissues of rainbow and moonshine."

In the same way, you are no longer the same since you became a follower of Christ. The basic structure of your personality and being is there, but your soul and spirit have come to life. At times you may still feel like the same hard, stiff person you were before; however, the Holy Spirit has come in. Your entire being is infused with the vivid presence of the Lord Jesus Christ. His holiness now flows through your veins. What was broken is whole. What was lost is found. What was dead is alive.

When you accept Christ as your Savior and invite Him into your heart and life, your body becomes a temple of the Holy Spirit (1 Corinthians 6:19). You undergo a miraculous spiritual rebirth and become a completely new creation (2 Corinthians 5:17). Because of your faith in Jesus, "rivers of living water" flow from deep within your heart (John 7:38 NIV). God is sanctifying you every day, remolding and making you, reshaping you in the image of Christ.

*And we all, who with unveiled faces contemplate*
*the Lord's glory, are being transformed into*
*his image with ever-increasing glory.*
2 CORINTHIANS 3:18 NIV

## Personal Application:

There's a big difference between living like an orphan and living like a member of God's family. As Christians, many of us still operate with an orphan mentality. When we're in trouble, we forget to call for help. When we're lost, we forget to stop and ask for directions. When we're in pain, we forget to ask for comfort and encouragement.

Do you live and operate like an orphan in your day-to-day life? Take time to journal through this question and reflect on how it applies to different areas of your life. You've been grafted into the family of God. Start living like you belong to Jesus. Meditate on today's scriptures and post them where you can see them. You are no longer a nobody from nowhere. You are a child of the God Most High.

## Prayer for Today:

*Jesus, I want to live like I belong to You. Please show me how to grasp the many great and precious promises I have in You. Holy Spirit, show me when and where I operate as an orphan and remind me to call on my Abba, Father in those moments. I especially need Your help in this area of my life: [Name the specific area]. In Jesus' name, amen.*

---

*He has granted to us his precious and very great promises, so that through them you may become partakers of the divine nature.*

2 Peter 1:4 esv

# Day 21
# A NEW DAY

---

*The steadfast love of the LORD never ceases;
his mercies never come to an end; they are
new every morning; great is your faithfulness.*
LAMENTATIONS 3:22–23 ESV

> "Marilla, isn't it nice to think that tomorrow is a new day with no mistakes in it yet?" (CH. 21)

In this chapter, Avonlea welcomes a new minister. Mr. and Mrs. Allan are a "young, pleasant-faced couple, still on their honeymoon, and full of all good and beautiful enthusiasms for their chosen lifework." The town opens "its heart to them from the start." Everyone likes the "frank, cheerful young man" and his "bright, gentle" wife. Even Anne, with her own astute opinions, declares Mr. Allan's sermon "interesting" and says he "prayed as if he meant it."

Anne also falls "promptly and wholeheartedly in love" with Mrs. Allan, "another kindred spirit." When Marilla invites Mr. and Mrs. Allan to tea, Anne is overjoyed. She bakes a cake as "light and feathery as golden foam" and decorates the tea table with an artistic "abundance of roses and ferns." However, when the cake tastes like anodyne liniment instead of vanilla, Anne "dissolve[s] into tears" and runs to her bedroom.

Anne fears she has made yet another bad first impression, but Mrs. Allan comes upstairs with her "merry voice" and "laughing eyes" and says "it's all just a funny mistake." She kindly asks to see Anne's flower garden and doesn't mention the cake again. Anne permits "herself to be led down and comforted, reflecting that it was really providential that Mrs. Allan was a kindred spirit." After the visit, a tired Anne tells Marilla it's "nice to think that tomorrow is a new day with no mistakes in it yet."

Tomorrow is a new day with no mistakes in it, but there will be mistakes in it at some point. No one is perfect. Every person is flawed. Everyone messes up, even if you never see it. In those moments, we need encouragement and help to move past our embarrassment and anguish. We don't need another Mrs. Lynde to judge or chide; we need a Mrs. Allan to comfort and cheer.

When we get mixed up, turned around, or immobilized by our past mistakes, the Bible reminds us of several truths to help us get up and continue moving forward. Every morning, God has new mercies waiting for you (Lamentations 3:22–23). You're in a constant state of being "renewed day by day" (2 Corinthians 4:16 NIV). When you feel weary, God promises to replenish your strength and make you "soar on wings like eagles" (Isaiah 40:31 NIV).

*One thing I do: forgetting what lies behind and straining forward to what lies ahead, I press on toward the goal for the prize of the upward call of God in Christ Jesus.*
PHILIPPIANS 3:13-14 ESV

# Personal Application:

What Anne doesn't realize is that this unfortunate baking fiasco marks the beginning of a long and fruitful friendship with Mrs. Allan. What a wonderful reminder that God often works in ways we don't expect, even using our mishaps and missteps to connect us with the people we need in our lives.

Do you feel like you need a new tomorrow—one with no mistakes in it? Do you look back with regret? Today is the day to make a fresh start. Whether you need a new beginning with your health, the way you use your time, or a difficult relationship, ask God for new mercies in your situation. If you struggle to let go of past mistakes, take this time to bring everything to the feet of Jesus and ask for His help to live a better tomorrow.

# Prayer for Today:

*Dear God, I'm so thankful for Your faithfulness.*
*You always steady my feet when I stumble and grant*
*me new strength when I'm weary. I confess to You my own*
*weaknesses and the sins of today: [Add your confession*
*here]. Please help me to start fresh in this area of my life:*
*[Name the specific area]. In Jesus' name, amen.*

---

*"Forget the former things; do not dwell on the past.*
*See, I am doing a new thing! Now it springs up;*
*do you not perceive it? I am making a way in the*
*wilderness and streams in the wasteland."*
Isaiah 43:18–19 niv

# Day 22
# A Heart-to-Heart Talk

*Whoever walks with the
wise becomes wise.*
PROVERBS 13:20 ESV

> "Mrs. Allan and I had a heart-to-heart talk. I told her everything—about Mrs. Thomas and the twins and Katie Maurice and Violetta and coming to Green Gables and my troubles over geometry." (CH. 22)

Mrs. Allan's arrival in Avonlea marks a new season in Anne's life. Though she's still young and still gets into plenty of scrapes, Anne is no longer a ragged little orphan girl trying to get by on her own gumption and smarts. At this point in the novel, she has spent a year soaking up the love, attention, training, and teaching of the people around her. Anne is starting to grow up. And now, at just the right time, she finds a spiritual mentor to guide her.

When Mrs. Allan invites Anne to tea at the manse, Anne stays afterward for a talk. When she comes home, she tells Marilla that she told Mrs. Allan "everything." They had a "heart-to-heart" talk about her life, her past, and her troubles. One can only imagine how that talk went, with Anne sharing her heart openly and Mrs. Allan listening kindly and compassionately, giving encouragement and gentle correction where needed.

Mrs. Allan joins Anne's support network just as Anne enters her teen years. She is someone Anne can talk to openly about her troubles, her worries, and her faith. She answers Anne's questions and helps her learn to follow God in her everyday life. Her example makes an immediate and lasting impact on Anne: "I never knew before that religion was such a cheerful thing. I always thought it was kind of melancholy, but Mrs. Allan's isn't, and I'd like to be a Christian if I could be one like her" (ch. 21).

We each play an important role in the family of God. Discipleship doesn't have to be formal, but it should be intentional. Jesus spent His days and nights walking, talking, and eating with His disciples. As they did ordinary, everyday things, Jesus taught them lessons about the kingdom of God. He showed them by example how to follow and serve God, how to help and heal others. And before He ascended into heaven, Jesus told His disciples to "go and make disciples of all nations" (Matthew 28:19 NIV). You have that same call on your life.

Throughout the Bible, we observe fascinating mentoring friendships. There's Paul and Timothy, Naomi and Ruth, Samuel and David. And in Titus 2, Paul says that men and women who are "older" in the faith should teach and train the younger men and women. Growth happens in community. We are meant to sharpen one another as "iron sharpens iron" (Proverbs 27:17 NIV). In the family of God, everyone has something to teach and everyone has something to learn.

*"Follow me and be my disciple," Jesus said to him. So Matthew got up and followed him.*
MATTHEW 9:9 NLT

## Personal Application:

Do you need a Mrs. Allan in your life? No matter your age, you need people who are a few steps ahead of you—practically and spiritually—to pour into your life and encourage you. If you don't have a spiritual mentor, start with prayer. It may not happen right away (or in the way you expect), but God will provide you with wise counselors.

God is also calling you to be a Mrs. Allan to a younger person in the faith. There are people around you who long to be mentored and helped in their walk with God. If you see someone treading paths you've already covered, reach back and lend a helping hand. Your encouragement and guidance can help him or her navigate a rocky patch.

## Prayer for Today:

*Lord Jesus, thank You for this reminder that I need healthy community in order to grow. Show me how to "go and make disciples" in my daily life. And lead me to wise, loving counselors who are a step ahead of me. I want to have a heart-to-heart chat with You about this area of my life: [Discuss specific area]. In Jesus' name, amen.*

*You shall teach them diligently to your children, and shall talk of them when you sit in your house, and when you walk by the way, and when you lie down, and when you rise.*

Deuteronomy 6:7 esv

# Day 23
# ON GOOD FIRM GROUND

―――――✳―――――

*Give careful thought to the paths for your feet
and be steadfast in all your ways. Do not turn
to the right or the left; keep your foot from evil.*
PROVERBS 4:26-27 NIV

> "But now [Marilla] knew as she hurried wildly down the slope that Anne was dearer to her than anything else on earth." (CH. 23)

In this chapter, Anne makes a rash decision that results in serious consequences. When Josie Pye dares Anne to walk the ridgepole of Mr. Barry's kitchen roof, Diana says she'll "fall off and be killed." Unfortunately, with her honor "at stake," Anne ignores Diana's warnings and says she'll walk the ridgepole or "perish in the attempt." After a few steps, she loses her balance and slides off the roof with a crash.

Later, when Anne asks Marilla what she would have done if she had been dared, Marilla says, "I'd have stayed on good firm ground and let them dare away." But Anne contends that she doesn't have Marilla's "strength of mind" and "couldn't bear Josie Pye's scorn." The truth is, Anne allowed her own pride and emotions to make her decision for her; she didn't stop to count the cost.

If Anne had "tumbled off the roof" on the steep side, she might have actually died. As it is, Ruby Gillis goes into hysterics,

Diana shrieks at the sight of Anne "lying all white and limp among the wreck and ruin," and Josie Pye is "seized with horrible visions" of Anne's "early and tragic death." Mr. and Mrs. Barry run to help, and when Marilla sees Mr. Barry carrying Anne, she experiences a "sudden stab of fear that pierce[s] her very heart." Anne herself suffers a painful broken ankle, misses seven weeks of school, and doesn't get to meet the new teacher.

There are many ridgepole moments in our lives—those times when we act without thinking or in response to an impulse or emotion. We get caught up in the moment, trying to prove ourselves or prove a point. Sometimes we even tread fine lines of morality, hoping we'll end up on the right side of things. We get swayed by other voices and entangle ourselves in messes. We rely a bit too much on God's grace to catch us when we fall.

We need to keep our feet firmly planted on the "good solid ground" of God's Word. The Bible tells us to build our lives on the solid rock of Christ (Matthew 7:24–27), keep to the paths of the righteous (Proverbs 2:20), and follow the way of wisdom (Proverbs 4:11). We're warned to avoid slippery slopes (Psalm 73:2), shifting sands (Matthew 7:26), and crooked paths (Isaiah 59:8). We find the right paths—paths of wisdom and instruction—in God's Word: "Your word is a lamp for my feet, a light on my path" (Psalm 119:105 NIV).

*The LORD makes firm the steps*
*of the one who delights in him.*
PSALM 37:23 NIV

## Personal Application:

The Bible says that a haughty spirit comes before a fall (Proverbs 16:18). In Anne's case, her pride causes a literal fall. Trying to navigate life without God is like trying to walk the ridgepole of a roof. We soon lose our balance and end up in a tangled mess. If you find yourself in a complicated situation, it's time to ask God to help.

Do you feel like you've wandered too far from God's paths or that your situation is too messy to fix? Nothing is impossible with God (Matthew 19:26). If you cry out to Jesus and ask for His forgiveness and help, He will cleanse you, forgive you, and set your feet on solid ground: "If we confess our sins, he is faithful and just to forgive us our sins and to cleanse us from all unrighteousness" (1 John 1:9 ESV).

## Prayer for Today:

*Lord, Jesus, I want to walk on Your paths. I sometimes live according to my ways instead of Your ways. Please shed light on my situation and show me where my pride is getting in the way. I ask now for Your Holy Spirit to guide me and make my crooked paths straight. [Add your prayer request.] In Jesus' name, amen.*

*He lifted me out of the slimy pit, out of the mud and mire; he set my feet on a rock and gave me a firm place to stand.*
Psalm 40:2 NIV

# Day 24
# THE SCHOOLHOUSE
# OF FAITH

---※---

*Day by day continuing with one mind in the temple,*
*and breaking bread from house to house, they were taking*
*their meals together with gladness and sincerity of heart.*
ACTS 2:46 NASB

> "Anne expanded like a flower under [Miss Stacy's] wholesome influence and carried home. . .glowing accounts of schoolwork and aims." (CH. 24)

In this chapter, Montgomery adds one more person to Anne's expanding circle of friends, family members, and mentors: Miss Stacy. Whereas Mr. Phillips wasn't "any good at all as a teacher" (ch. 15), Miss Stacy is a "bright, sympathetic young woman with the happy gift of winning and holding the affections of her pupils and bringing out the best that was in them mentally and morally." Anne finds "another true and helpful friend" in Miss Stacy (ch. 24).

Miss Stacy introduces physical education, nature studies, and field outings; puts on concerts; and later organizes a special Queen's prep course. She even makes geometry "clear" for Anne. Though some in Avonlea aren't sure about having their first "lady teacher," Miss Stacy soon proves herself as her students grow mentally, physically, and morally.

With Miss Stacy at the helm of Avonlea school, growth occurs at a steady pace. She makes learning enjoyable and inspires her students to challenge themselves and make discoveries. She provides solid mental and moral instruction. Where there were once uneven, undisciplined studies in the little schoolhouse, there is now consistent growth: "Work in Miss Stacy's little kingdom went on with regularity and smoothness" (ch. 26).

The picture of the happy schoolhouse, humming along pleasantly, provides insight for us spiritually. In our own schoolhouse of faith, we start by choosing to follow Jesus, our Teacher, the One who holds our affections and brings out the best in us. We learn from Him, for He is "gentle and humble in heart"; in Him, we find "rest" for our souls (Matthew 11:29 NIV). We also have earthly teachers: "the apostles, the prophets, the evangelists, the shepherds and teachers" who help "equip the saints for the work of ministry, for building up the body of Christ" (Ephesians 4:11–12 ESV).

As Christ's followers, we engage in a wide range of spiritual disciplines that help us love God with all our heart, soul, and strength (Deuteronomy 6:5). We read, study, and reason. We worship, meditate, and pray. We love, give, and serve. As members of Christ's body, we also regularly gather and grow with other Christians: "They devoted themselves to the apostles' teaching and to fellowship, to the breaking of bread and to prayer" (Acts 2:42 NIV). These are the building blocks of steady spiritual growth.

*As you received Christ Jesus the Lord, so walk in him,*
*rooted and built up in him and established in the faith,*
*just as you were taught, abounding in thanksgiving.*
COLOSSIANS 2:6-7 ESV

## PERSONAL APPLICATION:

How would you rate your personal schoolhouse of faith? Is there an area of your spiritual life that is uneven or underdeveloped? Your spiritual curriculum includes personal Bible study and prayer, sound biblical teaching, church attendance, and Christian fellowship and service. Neglecting any of these areas can hamper the "regularity and smoothness" of your spiritual growth.

Finally, in Miss Stacy's well-regulated little school, "trifling frictions" between students are the only hiccups along the way (ch. 26). What a great exhortation to live in harmony with other believers! As believers, we have to be on our guard, because a little bit of friction can cause a giant chasm. If you have even a small conflict with someone, or if bigger issues have become a stumbling block, it's time to confess, repent, forgive, and recommit.

## PRAYER FOR TODAY:

*Dear Jesus, please be my Teacher in the schoolhouse of faith. I want to grow in my faith with smoothness and regularity. Guard my heart against trifling frictions with others. Please help me grow in the areas of my spiritual life that are stagnant or sagging. [Add your prayer request.] In Jesus' name, amen.*

---

*How good and pleasant it is when God's people live together in unity! It is like precious oil poured on the head, running down on the beard, running down on Aaron's beard, down on the collar of his robe.*

Psalm 133:1–2 NIV

# Day 25
# ABBA, FATHER

—※—

*Those who seek the L<small>ORD</small> lack no good thing.*
P<small>SALM</small> 34:10 <small>NIV</small>

> "Anne took the dress and looked at it in reverent silence. 'That's a Christmas present for you, Anne,' said Matthew shyly." (CH. 25)

When Matthew observes Anne with her friends, he takes careful note of her "brighter face, and bigger, starrier eyes, and more delicate features." But he's puzzled to discover that there's something different about her appearance. Somehow she doesn't quite fit in. After two hours of "hard reflection," he finally realizes what it is: Anne isn't "dressed like the other girls." He thinks that it won't cause any harm to "let the child have one pretty dress" and decides to do something about it himself.

Getting a dress for Anne is quite a "gruesome experience" for Matthew, but he's determined to do it. He immediately rules out Marilla. He decides to try the local store but comes back with a garden rake, twenty pounds of brown sugar, and no dress. Finally, he asks Mrs. Lynde to sew it, "for of no other woman in Avonlea" would he dare "to ask advice." Once it's settled, he goes around "looking so mysterious. . .and grinning" to himself for two weeks.

Dear Matthew loves Anne so well. He actively thinks about what she might like or want, going beyond her immediate needs to the special little gifts that bless her with abundance and joy. He gives her a "perfectly exquisite" dress for Christmas—complete with "dainty frills and shirrings," an "elaborately pintucked" waist, a "little ruffle of filmy lace at the neck," and beautiful puffed sleeves. And at the end of the chapter, he tells Marilla about something else he has noticed: Anne will "need something more than Avonlea school by and by."

Matthew's attentiveness to Anne's needs gives us a glimpse into the overwhelming Father-love God has for us as His children. He anticipates and meets our needs each day, working behind the scenes in ways we cannot imagine. He goes further than our immediate necessities and does "far more abundantly than all that we ask or think" (Ephesians 3:20 ESV). He loves to give good gifts to His children and provides us with tangible reminders of His presence, protection, and love.

The Bible says, "See what great love the Father has lavished on us, that we should be called children of God! And that is what we are!" (1 John 3:1 NIV). We can actually see and experience God's love at work in our lives. We see it in Christ, the image of God, through the way He lived His life. We see it in His sacrifice on the cross, to purchase our salvation. And we see it in our adoption: God gave His only Son so that we could become children of God (John 3:16).

*Every good and perfect gift is from above,*
*coming down from the Father of the heavenly*
*lights, who does not change like shifting shadows.*
JAMES 1:17 NIV

## PERSONAL APPLICATION:

In chapter 11, Anne whispers, "I prayed for [a dress with puffed sleeves], but I didn't much expect it on that account. I didn't suppose God would have time to bother about a little orphan girl's dress." Have you ever supposed something similar about your Father in heaven? Here's the truth: He *does* have time. He *does* bother over you. And He *does* care about the little details of your life.

Romans 8:15 (NLT) says this: "You have not received a spirit that makes you fearful slaves. Instead, you received God's Spirit when he adopted you as his own children. Now we call him 'Abba, Father.' " As God's own child, you have nothing to fear; you can go to Him with any problem or request! He is your good and loving Father who "knows what you need before you ask" (Matthew 6:8 ESV).

## PRAYER FOR TODAY:

*Abba, Father, thank You for caring for me and for noticing my needs. You always go above and beyond all I could ask or think. Open my eyes to the tangible reminders of Your love all around me. I ask now for Your provision in this area of my life: [Name the specific area]. In Jesus' name, amen.*

---

*"If God so clothes the grass, which is alive in the field today, and tomorrow is thrown into the oven, how much more will he clothe you, O you of little faith!"*
LUKE 12:28 ESV

# Day 26
# EVERYDAY FAITHFULNESS

---*---

*Trust in the LORD and do good; dwell in
the land and cultivate faithfulness.*
PSALM 37:3 NASB

> "Junior Avonlea found it hard to settle down to humdrum existence again. To Anne in particular things seemed fearfully flat, stale, and unprofitable after the goblet of excitement she had been sipping for weeks." (CH. 26)

After the excitement of the school concert, Anne wonders if she can ever go back to "the former quiet pleasures of those faraway days before the concert." She tells Diana that life "can never be quite the same again." Though she figures she'll eventually get used to regular life once more, Anne fears Marilla might be right about concerts spoiling people "for everyday life."

After a time, life does get back to normal. The school slips back into its "old groove" with all its "old interests," and Anne and her friends form a story club. Marilla calls the story club foolish, Mr. and Mrs. Allan laugh "at all the wrong places," and Aunt Josephine says she "never read anything so amusing in her life." But Anne thinks that their stories must be "doing some good in the world," which Mrs. Allan says is one of the highest goals in life.

At age thirteen, Anne is beginning to think more philosophically about her actions and interests. She now gives her fanciful stories a "good moral" and tries for a "wholesome effect." She strives to be "a little like Mrs. Allan" when she grows up, even though Marilla says Anne is "silly" and "forgetful." And little by little, she's learning everyday faithfulness as she studies, does her chores, says her prayers, and goes to church.

There are many occasions when it's hard to settle down and enjoy the "humdrum" parts of life. Weekends, vacations, and holidays are much more fun than school, work, or chores. However, humdrum days make up a far greater part of our lives than special days. Our stories unfold on ordinary days. It's in the doing, in the journey, in the day-to-day that we learn the best lessons and grow the most. That's when *life* happens. That's when God does a gradual and continual work to mold and shape us into the image of Christ. And that's when we have the opportunity to do the most "good" in the world.

God's greatest, most profound, and often most difficult call on our lives is everyday faithfulness. The Bible tells us that you and I are "God's handiwork, created in Christ Jesus to do good works, which God prepared in advance for us to do" (Ephesians 2:10 NIV). This verse isn't merely referring to momentous works, ministries, or missions. It's referring to the good works God has planned for us to do in our everyday lives, in a laundry room, in an office, in a classroom, or at a cash register.

> *"One who is faithful in a very little is also faithful in much."*
> LUKE 16:10 ESV

# PERSONAL APPLICATION:

Faithfulness doesn't happen overnight. Your life is like a tapestry. It's hard to see the big picture when you're weaving together small threads, but remember that God can see the entire design from start to finish. As you seek to "do some good" in the lives of your friends, family, and coworkers, God is at work.

Don't discount the small deposits you make each day. The first few months of around-the-clock diaper changes, feedings, and lullabies form a bond between a mother and infant that lasts a lifetime. Years of monotonous scales, theory, and practice make a novice into a pianist. Decades of dedication take a simple idea and transform it into a flourishing business. Take time now to ask God to make your *daily* appointments into *divine* appointments.

# PRAYER FOR TODAY:

*Lord Jesus, thank You that You are always faithful. I want to see the sacred in the mundane. Open my eyes to the beauty You're weaving in and through my life. Help me to show up for people, be present, and do good to those around me today. I want to grow in everyday faithfulness in this area: [Name the specific area]. In Jesus' name, amen.*

*Let not steadfast love and faithfulness forsake you; bind them around your neck; write them on the tablet of your heart.*
PROVERBS 3:3 ESV

# Day 27
# BLIND SPOTS

---

*Point out anything in me that offends you,*
*and lead me along the path of everlasting life.*
PSALM 139:24 NLT

> "I never thought I was vain about my hair, of all things, but now I know I was, in spite of its being red, because it was so long and thick and curly." (CH. 27)

In the previous chapter, Anne talked to Mrs. Allan about "beset-ting sins" and discovered that hers was "imagining too much and forgetting [her] duties." She is growing up and "striving very hard to overcome" her faults. However, there's something she has yet to learn about herself: her obsession with her looks—and especially her hair—is perhaps an even bigger stumbling block than her overactive imagination.

When Anne first meets Matthew, she says she can't "feel exactly perfectly happy" because of her red hair, sighing over it in a way that seems "to exhale forth all the sorrows of the ages" (ch. 2). She tells Marilla she never prays because she believes God made her hair red on purpose (ch. 7). When Mrs. Lynde says her hair is "as red as carrots," Anne screams at her, "head up, eyes blazing, hands clenched" (ch. 9). And when Gilbert calls her "Carrots," she smashes her slate over his head and refuses to talk to him for five years.

It's no wonder the bottle of hair dye in the peddler's box

is "irresistible" to Anne (ch. 27). She has always wanted to be "divinely beautiful." The only compliment she has ever received is about her nose, which hardly outweighs all the criticism she has heard. Anne has good reason to be self-conscious about her looks. However, when her hair turns green and Marilla has to cut it off, Anne discovers that she's far more vain than she realized.

Anne doesn't recognize her problem until she looks in the mirror. In much the same way, we often can't see the giant stumbling blocks in our own lives. Some of our deepest issues hide out in plain sight. They often come under the guise of attitudes, behaviors, and coping mechanisms—some of which even seem quite reasonable at first glance. That's why we need God's Word: reading it is like putting a mirror up to our lives. As we lay our desires, motives, outbursts, and behavior alongside the truth and wisdom of the Bible, we see our true selves.

King David was blind to his sin when he committed adultery with Bathsheba and murdered her husband, Uriah. Thankfully, God sent the prophet Nathan to help open David's eyes. He told David a parable about a rich man who took a poor man's only sheep. When David burst out in anger at the story, Nathan said David had done the same and worse: "You struck down Uriah the Hittite with the sword and took his wife to be your own" (2 Samuel 12:9 NIV). David immediately confessed, "I have sinned against the LORD" (2 Samuel 12:13 NIV).

> *How can I know all the sins lurking in my heart?*
> *Cleanse me from these hidden faults.*
> PSALM 19:12 NLT

## PERSONAL APPLICATION:

We all have blind spots. When left unattended, even seemingly small issues can grow into giant stumbling blocks. Like icebergs, what's visible on the surface is often only a symptom of something bigger that's going on below the surface. The bravest thing we can do is ask God to show us our blind spots and open our ears to what He wants to say.

The things we're most sensitive about act as a cover for deeper issues. Our hang-ups can erode relationships and control how we act and think. Ask God to show you what you can't see. And in light of your own insecurities, go easy on the people around you. Every person has sore spots. In love, you can lift burdens, shine light, and give grace.

## PRAYER FOR TODAY:

*Lord Jesus, please open my eyes to my blind spots. Show me what I can't see about myself and my relationships. Give me new eyes to see my own sensitivities and trigger points. I want to get down to the root causes. Please be my gentle Shepherd as I process these issues. [Add your prayer request.] In Jesus' name, amen.*

---

*For the word of God is alive and powerful. It is sharper than the sharpest two-edged sword, cutting between soul and spirit, between joint and marrow. It exposes our innermost thoughts and desires.*
HEBREWS 4:12 NLT

# Day 28
# OLD GRIEVANCES

---

*Let all bitterness and wrath and anger
and clamor and slander be put away
from you, along with all malice.*
EPHESIANS 4:31 ESV

> "The bitterness of [Anne's] old grievance promptly stiffened up her wavering determination. . . . She hated Gilbert Blythe! She would never forgive him!" (CH. 28)

In this chapter, Anne plays "Lily Maid" and accidentally sinks the Barrys' boat. As she clings to the slippery pilings under the bridge and prays desperately for help, Gilbert rows by and rescues her. At the landing, he lays a hand on her arm and says, "Can't we be good friends? I'm awfully sorry I made fun of your hair that time. . . . I think your hair is awfully pretty now—honest I do. Let's be friends."

This is Anne's golden opportunity to forgive Gilbert. When she sees the "half-shy, half-eager expression" in his hazel eyes, her heart gives a "quick, queer little beat." She hesitates, but "the bitterness of her old grievance" raises its ugly head and she refuses his offer of friendship. Gilbert says he'll never ask again and rows away with an "angry color in his cheeks." Anne immediately regrets her horrible words and later reflects that "she would answer very differently" if she could do it over again (ch. 30).

Gilbert once wronged Anne, but now she's in the wrong. He has done everything he can to win her over, but she has repaid his kindness with scorn one too many times. This rift is no longer about Gilbert, the bad guy; it's about Anne, the resentful, the unforgiving, the cruel. As a result, her stubbornness creates an even greater chasm. From this point on, there's "open rivalry" between them; Gilbert ignores her, evincing "no recognition whatever of the existence of Anne Shirley" (ch. 30).

When we hold on to resentment and grudges, we end up hurting ourselves more than anyone else. Precious opportunities slip by and relationships sour. What's more, bitterness and anger run contrary to the heart of our heavenly Father, for He is a "God of forgiveness, gracious and compassionate, slow to anger and abounding in lovingkindness" (Nehemiah 9:17 NASB).

Ecclesiastes 3 (NIV) says there's a proper time for everything. It explains the ebb and flow of life with its ups and downs, gains and losses. It says there's a "time to tear down and a time to build" (v. 3), a "time to tear and a time to mend" (v. 7), and a "time for war and a time for peace" (v. 8). Kindred spirit, the proper time to build bridges, mend broken hearts, and make peace is *right now*. Not tomorrow, not "someday," but today.

> *Make allowance for each other's faults, and forgive*
> *anyone who offends you. Remember, the Lord*
> *forgave you, so you must forgive others.*
> COLOSSIANS 3:13 NLT

## PERSONAL APPLICATION:

Today is your golden opportunity to live free. Jesus came to "proclaim liberty to the captives" (Luke 4:18 ESV). In Christ you now "walk in the newness of life" (Romans 6:4 ESV). He has set you free from sin and death and *every* other thing that holds you in its grip—including bitterness and unforgiveness. He invites you to release your anger and resentment into His hands and receive healing from the inside out.

Our God is a God of second chances. If there's anything hindering your walk with Him or affecting your relationships, it's time to let go and confess that bitter root today. If you've been wounded by another person, take this time to pray for God's help to choose forgiveness.

## PRAYER FOR TODAY:

*Dearest Jesus, thank You for loving me and for saving me. I want to please You with my thoughts, words, and actions. Help me live in my new identity and let go of the past. Please heal my wounded heart. Please take my grievances and remove the bitter root in this area of my life: [Name the specific area]. In Jesus' name, amen.*

---

*See to it that no one falls short of the grace of God and that no bitter root grows up to cause trouble and defile many.*
HEBREWS 12:15 NIV

# Day 29
## BELONGING

*We are his people, and the sheep of his pasture.*
PSALM 100:3 ESV

> "It's nice to be eating ice cream at brilliant restaurants at eleven o'clock at night once in a while; but as a regular thing I'd rather be in the east gable at eleven, sound asleep, but kind of knowing even in my sleep that the stars were shining outside and that the wind was blowing in the firs across the brook." (CH. 29)

In this chapter, Anne and Diana travel to visit Miss Barry and attend the Exhibition. Their time in town "from first to last" is "crowded with delights." Miss Barry's house is luxurious with its velvet carpets, silk curtains, and beautiful spare room. They visit the Exhibition grounds, drive in the park, listen to a concert by a prima donna, and eat ice cream in a restaurant late at night.

The only problem: there's no "scope for the imagination." Anne feels insignificant in the big city, she's too excited to sleep, and spare rooms don't quite live up to the hype: "That's the worst of growing up, and I'm beginning to realize it. The things you wanted so much when you were a child don't seem half so wonderful to you when you get them." Anne concludes that the "best of it all was the coming home."

Anne realizes she wasn't "born for city life" and is "glad of it." She likes visiting in town, but she *belongs* at Green Gables. Miss Barry says she'd be a "better and happier woman" with someone like Anne in the house. And when Anne gets home, Marilla shares a similar sentiment: "It's been fearful lonesome here without you, and I never put in four longer days."

Each of us has a place where we belong. First, God designed us to be part of His family. Apart from Him, we wander—lonely, isolated, and lost. In God's family, we have full rights as His heirs and access to God's throne of grace. Second, we all have a place where we belong in the body of Christ, among our brothers and sisters. Finally, we also each have an actual location—a specific address—where we belong.

God has planted you where you are for a reason. We see this illustrated in Mark 5, when Jesus freed a man possessed by demons. Once the man was seated and in his right mind, he begged Jesus to let him go with Him on His travels, but Jesus had a better plan: He told the man to stay home and tell everyone there about what God had done for him. The man stayed and shared his testimony with everyone in the area, and they were *all* amazed.

> *"Go home to your people and report to them*
> *what great things the Lord has done for you,*
> *and how He had mercy on you."*
> MARK 5:19 NASB

## PERSONAL APPLICATION:

Jesus wants to work through you to reach the people you interact with regularly. Though He sometimes calls us to move to a different neighborhood, city, or country, He always wants us to love the people around us. Wherever you are today—at home, at work or school, at the doctor's office—that's exactly where God wants you to be.

It may seem as though another life or another location would seem better or brighter, but God has purposes for you right here, right now. Jesus wants you to tell people about *all* that the Lord has done for you. Pray for divine appointments this week, and be ready to share one of your own "Jesus stories." Your personal testimony is one of the most powerful things you can share.

## PRAYER FOR TODAY:

*Dear God, thank You that I belong to You and that You've brought me to this exact place and time on earth for a purpose. Please use my life to impact the people around me each day in the way I talk and act. Help me share one of my Jesus stories with someone this week. [Add your prayer request.] In Jesus' name, amen.*

---

*This world is not our permanent home;
we are looking forward to a home yet to come.*
HEBREWS 13:14 NLT

# Day 30
# CIRCLES OF INFLUENCE

*And the boy Samuel continued to grow in stature
and in favor with the LORD and with people.*
1 SAMUEL 2:26 NIV

> "[Anne] was happy, eager, interested; there were lessons to be learned and honor to be won; delightful books to read; new pieces to be practiced for the Sunday-school choir; pleasant Saturday afternoons at the manse with Mrs. Allan." (CH. 30)

In this chapter, Anne joins Miss Stacy's Queen's preparation course. Along the way, we get a detailed glimpse into Anne's character growth and her circle of influencers. She and Diana begin to "talk a great deal about serious subjects." Mrs. Rachel Lynde says Anne has become "a real smart girl." And Marilla says Anne is "real steady and reliable"; she can "trust her in anything."

Anne listens carefully when Miss Stacy takes the teen girls to the brook for a talk: "She said we couldn't be too careful what habits we formed and what ideals we acquired in our teens, because by the time we were twenty our characters would be developed and the foundation laid for our whole future life." On the way home, she and Diana decide to form "respectable habits" and be "as sensible as possible."

And Anne isn't all talk; there is visible evidence of an inward change. At the horse races, Anne refuses to place a bet because she wants to be able to tell Mrs. Allan everything: "It's as good as an extra conscience to have a minister's wife for your friend" (ch. 29). She won't "read any book now unless either Miss Stacy or Mrs. Allan thinks it is a proper book." And she's trying to "overcome" her talkative nature: "If you only knew how many things I want to say and don't, you'd give me some credit for it."

We all have a circle of influencers in our lives, from our family, friends, classmates, and coworkers to what we read, watch, and listen to on a daily basis. We don't have a say about some of the influences in our lives, but we do get to choose how we spend our free time, whom we hang around, and what messages we digest. Just as "bad company corrupts good morals" (1 Corinthians 15:33 NASB), so good company encourages good character.

When Daniel was taken to Babylon as a slave (Daniel 1), he was given a Babylonian name and education. He was surrounded by pagan images and messages each day. He didn't have a say about his daily work, what he heard, or what he saw, but he made two important choices: he selected his companions wisely by spending time with three other young Hebrew men who were faithful to God (Daniel 1), and he used his time wisely by going to his room to pray three times a day (Daniel 6).

> *[Daniel] got down on his knees three times*
> *a day and prayed and gave thanks before*
> *his God, as he had done previously.*
> DANIEL 6:10 ESV

## PERSONAL APPLICATION:

Who is in your circle of influencers? Consider your friends, your mentors, your teachers, and your family members. Now think about the influencers you don't personally know, such as people on TV shows or podcasts you enjoy, authors and publishers of books and magazines you read, and singers and songwriters you listen to on the radio.

We're bombarded with positive and negative messages every day. We can either gather wisdom from godly sources or listen to worldly ideas. Some messages we hear are blatant, while others are subtle. It's important to be selective about the information we pump into our minds, ears, eyes, and hearts each day. We must become our own censors. Finally, we need to choose our friends and mentors wisely and renew our minds daily through Bible study and prayer.

## PRAYER FOR TODAY:

*Lord, thank You for reminding me that I hear a multitude of messages and voices each day. Please give me wisdom and discernment about what I listen to, watch, and read. Provide me with wise mentors and godly companions. Show me which influences I need to avoid and which influences I need to pursue. [Add your prayer request.] In Jesus' name, amen.*

---

*Do not conform to the pattern of this world,*
*but be transformed by the renewing of your mind.*
ROMANS 12:2 NIV

# Day 31
# QUIET MY SOUL

---

*Let your adorning be the hidden person of the heart
with the imperishable beauty of a gentle and quiet
spirit, which in God's sight is very precious.*
1 PETER 3:4 ESV

> "It's a serious thing to grow up, isn't it, Marilla? But when I have such good friends as you and Matthew and Mrs. Allan and Miss Stacy I ought to grow up successfully, and I'm sure it will be my own fault if I don't. I feel it's a great responsibility because I have only the one chance." (CH. 31)

Anne is swiftly growing into a young lady. Marilla is astonished to discover as they stand side by side one day that Anne is now taller than she is. She feels a "queer regret" because she feels that the "child she had learned to love had vanished somehow and here was this tall, serious-eyed girl of fifteen, with the thoughtful brows and the proudly poised little head, in her place."

Anne is learning to buckle down and work. She understands that there's a time to dream and a time to focus. In fact, she studies so hard that the Spencervale doctor sends Marilla a message: "Keep that redheaded girl of yours in the open air all summer and don't let her read books until she gets more spring into her step." Marilla takes it to heart and makes sure Anne has a "golden summer" with plenty of walking, rowing, berrying, and dreaming.

Marilla also notices that Anne is quieter and more thoughtful now: "You don't chatter half as much as you used to, Anne, nor use half as many big words. What has come over you?" Anne blushes and looks "dreamily out of the window." She finally says she doesn't talk as much because it's "nicer to think dear, pretty thoughts and keep them in one's heart, like treasures."

Cultivating a gentle, quiet spirit is "precious" in God's sight (1 Peter 3:4 ESV). Sometimes it's wonderful to share our thoughts, desires, worries, and concerns with others. But there's something special about spending time in quiet reflection in order to think things over with God. We can bring Him our fears and anxieties. We can ask His advice about decisions. And we can reflect and rejoice over the wonderful things He has done.

In Luke 2 (ESV), angels appeared to a group of shepherds during the night and told them of Jesus' birth. They ran to find Jesus and told Joseph and Mary what the angels had said: "For unto you is born this day in the city of David a Savior, who is Christ the Lord" (v. 11). When Mary heard their amazing message, she didn't erupt in a frenzy of questions, excitement, and chatter; instead, she "treasured up all these things, pondering them in her heart" (v. 19).

*Rest in God alone, my soul,*
*for my hope comes from Him.*
PSALM 62:5 HCSB

## Personal Application:

Is your soul healthy and well-nourished? The psalmist describes his soul like this: "I have calmed and quieted my soul, like a weaned child with its mother; like a weaned child is my soul within me" (Psalm 131:2 ESV). Isn't that a beautiful picture? Now think about what it would be like if your soul was content, quiet, happy, and well-fed.

Soul care is an important part of your walk with Christ. To have a gentle, quiet spirit doesn't mean you change your personality or become weak or ineffectual. It means that you're ruled by Christ's gentle nature. In your heart, there's a stillness—a settled knowledge that God is in charge (Psalm 46:10). Take this time to ask God to calm and quiet your soul.

## Prayer for Today:

*Lord Jesus, thank You for saving me. I praise You that my soul is reborn, that my heart is at rest, that You're in charge. I confess that the words of my mouth and the meditations of my heart aren't always pleasing to You. I want a gentle, quiet spirit. Please take these heavy burdens I'm carrying and give me rest. [Add your prayer request.] In Jesus' name, amen.*

---

*May the words of my mouth and the meditation of my heart be pleasing to you, O Lord, my rock and my redeemer.*
Psalm 19:14 NLT

# Day 32
# REJOICING

---

*Rejoice with those who rejoice,*
*weep with those who weep.*
ROMANS 12:15 ESV

> " 'I'll write Tuesday night and tell you how the first day goes,' promised Anne. 'I'll be haunting the post office Wednesday,' vowed Diana." (CH. 32)

Though she giggled at the time, Diana was serious when she vowed to be faithful to her bosom friend, Anne, for "as long as the sun and moon shall endure." Diana is always there for Anne—cheering her on, hoping for the best, and taking great pride in her accomplishments. They share books, give gifts, and sit together at school. She's a "faithful" (ch. 23) and "very comfortable sort of friend" (ch. 21). She rejoices when Anne rejoices and weeps when she weeps.

After the red currant wine episode, Diana tells Anne, "I love you devotedly, Anne. . .and I always will, you may be sure of that" (ch. 17). She belongs to "Matthew's school of critics" (ch. 26). She "alone of outsiders [knows] the fatal secret" about Anne's green hair and promises "never to tell" (ch. 27). And when she thinks Anne might be killed—twice!—she's frantic at the thought of losing her best friend. Most touching of all is Diana's unflagging support for her friend as Anne pursues the education Diana's parents won't let her have.

Through all the years of studies, classes, and long hours, Diana encourages Anne. She haunts the post office and waits for news when Anne takes her entrance exams. She's waiting at Green Gables when Anne returns home afterward. And when the pass results come out, Diana comes "flying" over to Green Gables with them. She bursts into Anne's room without knocking, "so great [is] her excitement" to share the good news that Anne tied for first. She tells Anne, "Oh, I'm so proud!" and collapses on the bed.

It's a true friend, indeed, who not only weeps with you when you weep but also rejoices with you when you rejoice. When a friend is down in the dumps, loses a loved one, or is in great difficulty, it's natural to want to comfort and console her. It's also easy to rejoice with others when your life is sunny. But when something wonderful happens to a friend, especially if you're going through a rough patch or if you're struggling with an unmet need, it's not quite as simple. Sometimes it can be a real sacrifice to lay aside your own feelings and truly rejoice when your friends get great news.

In the Old Testament, Jonathan was a steadfast friend to David. As King Saul's eldest son, Jonathan was heir to the throne of Israel. However, when it became clear that David was God's choice as the next king, Jonathan remained loyal to David. He didn't fight for his right to the throne; instead, he spoke on David's behalf to Saul and saved his life. He told David, "You will be king over Israel, and I will be second to you" (1 Samuel 23:17 NIV).

*Love bears all things, believes all things,*
*hopes all things, endures all things.*
1 CORINTHIANS 13:7 ESV

## Personal Application:

It's far more enjoyable to be the Anne character who is experiencing great success than the Diana character who is cheering from the sidelines. However, God challenges us to cry when our friends cry and jump for joy when they get good news. When it's a struggle to join in cheerfully, it's because something is amiss in our hearts and needs immediate tending.

If you find it hard to rejoice with those you love, take this time to bare your heart before the Lord and ask Him to give you His great love for your friends. If you find it difficult to come alongside and be compassionate or sympathetic when your friends are in pain, take this time to ask the Lord to do a work in your heart to nurture a spirit of compassion.

## Prayer for Today:

*Lord Jesus, I want to be more like You. I want to be there for my friends and family members with a pure heart. Help me to grow in the area of comforting those who mourn. Remind me to join in the party wholeheartedly and praise You when my friends experience joy. Please help me to be a better friend to these people: [Add names here]. In Jesus' name, amen.*

---

*A friend loves at all times.*
Proverbs 17:17 esv

# Day 33
# RICH INDEED

*I pray that the eyes of your heart may be
enlightened in order that you may know the
hope to which he has called you, the riches of
his glorious inheritance in his holy people.*
EPHESIANS 1:18 NIV

**"**

> " 'We are rich,' said Anne staunchly.
> 'Why, we have sixteen years to our credit,
> and we're happy as queens, and we've all
> got imaginations, more or less.' " (CH. 33)

**"**

At the White Sands hotel concert, Anne learns an important lesson about riches. Upon arriving, she feels "suddenly shy and frightened and countrified." Her dress, "which, in the east gable, had seemed so dainty and pretty," now seems "too simple and plain. . .among all the silks and laces that [glisten] and [rustle] around her." Her "pearl beads" don't compare to the flashy diamonds, and her "wee white rose" looks poor "beside all the hothouse flowers." She shrinks "miserably into a corner" and wishes herself "back in the white room at Green Gables."

On stage, the "electric lights [dazzle] her eyes, the perfume and hum [bewilder] her." When it's her turn, Anne has "an overwhelming attack of stage fright." The sight of the audience "paralyze[s] her energies completely." Everything seems "so strange, so brilliant, so bewildering." She misses the "homely, sympathetic faces of friends and neighbors." She finally rises to the occasion but only because she believes (incorrectly) that

Gilbert is taunting her.

Afterward, however, Anne comes to an important conclusion. Her friend Jane says she wishes she could wear "jewels and low-necked dresses and have ice cream and chicken salad every blessed day," but Anne argues that they *are* rich already. She doesn't think "millions of dollars" or "ropes of diamonds" result in true happiness. She says, "I'm quite content to be Anne of Green Gables, with my string of pearl beads. I know Matthew gave me as much love with them as ever went with Madame the Pink Lady's jewels."

It's tempting to look at the people around us and wonder if we're missing something. As Christians there are times when we might seem backward or out of fashion in comparison with the way others live and think. The world values flashy signs of material wealth, success, and power much more than moral fiber and integrity. But remember that God looks at the heart (1 Samuel 16:7). When we focus our attention on Jesus and on sharing His love with others, we discover deep wells of contentment and joy.

The Bible tells us that true riches aren't visible to the naked eye. Paul wrote this to the Philippians: "Indeed, I count everything as loss because of the *surpassing worth of knowing Christ Jesus my Lord*" (Philippians 3:8 ESV, emphasis added). In Christ you have eternal salvation and a heavenly inheritance—a spiritual inheritance that is "imperishable, undefiled, and unfading, kept in heaven for you" (1 Peter 1:4 ESV). Knowing Jesus means incomparable treasure now and forever.

*"Lay up for yourselves treasure in heaven, where neither moth nor rust destroys and where thieves do not break in and steal."*
MATTHEW 6:20 ESV

## PERSONAL APPLICATION:

How often do you find yourself looking at others and wishing you could have what they have, do what they do, or enjoy the opportunities they've been given? It's important that you and I remember two things: first, everyone has their battles; and second, when we compare ourselves to others, we quickly become discontented with our own lot.

Take this time today to write down a list of the riches you have in Christ and the many blessings you enjoy in your life. Thank God for what you *do* have and shift your focus off of what you *don't* have. For those deep and unmet desires that you know God has placed on your heart for a purpose, don't give up. Keep your eyes on Christ as you wait.

## PRAYER FOR TODAY:

*Heavenly Father, thank You for inviting me into Your family and making me Your own. I confess I'm discontented and discouraged at times. Please show me how to invest in eternal things today. I thank and praise You for the great riches You've bestowed on me. [List specific blessings you are thankful for.] In Jesus' name, amen.*

---

*A good name is more desirable than great riches; to be esteemed is better than silver or gold.*
PROVERBS 22:1 NIV

# Day 34
# PRUNED AND BLOOMING

---

*"Your Father knows what you
need before you ask him."*
MATTHEW 6:8 ESV

> "I'm not a bit changed—not really. I'm only just pruned down and branched out. The real me—back here—is just the same." (CH. 34)

In the final weeks before Anne leaves for Queen's, we're given the opportunity to reflect on the fruit of the providential "mistake" that brought her to Green Gables. There are physical changes, such as the east gable that's now "as sweet and dainty a nest as a young girl could desire" (ch. 33), but the people are altered as well. Anne isn't the only one "pruned down and branched out." While Anne grew up, Matthew and Marilla blossomed too.

As Marilla thinks back on Anne's arrival, tears fill her eyes. She remembers the "vivid picture of the odd, frightened child in her preposterous yellowish-brown wincey dress, the heartbreak looking out of her tearful eyes." She puts "her arms close about her girl and hold[s] her tenderly to her heart, wishing that she need never let her go." After Anne departs, Marilla plunges "fiercely into unnecessary work" and keeps at it "all day long with the bitterest kind of heartache." That night she's "acutely and miserably conscious" of Anne's empty room, and she weeps "for her girl in a passion of sobs."

Similarly there's a "suspicious moisture" in Matthew's eyes as well as he considers how smart, pretty, and loving Anne has grown to be. He gives God credit for bringing Anne to Green Gables: "She's been a blessing to us, and there never was a luckier mistake than what Mrs. Spencer made—if it was luck. I don't believe it was any such thing. It was Providence, because the Almighty saw we needed her, I reckon." He thinks that putting in his "oar" when it came to bringing up Anne "never did much harm after all."

We must be pruned in order to grow. Just as the "Almighty" *knew* Matthew and Marilla needed Anne, so God works providentially in your life. He knows the desires of your heart and tends your heart with care; He wisely gives you what you need most and tenderly takes away what's harmful. He prunes us down as a loving vinedresser, trimming back the old, making room for new growth, and encouraging us to branch out.

In the New Testament, Peter is an example of someone who was pruned back so he could branch out. A brave and brawny fisherman, he told Jesus he would never leave His side even if it meant his own death. But when Jesus was betrayed, Peter denied even knowing Him—three times. After the resurrection, Jesus went to Peter, gave him the opportunity to renew his allegiance, and told him to feed His sheep (John 21:15–17). A softer, gentler Peter became the apostle to the Jews and built an incredibly fruitful legacy (Galatians 2:8).

> *"Every branch in me that does not bear fruit he takes away, and every branch that does bear fruit he prunes, that it may bear more fruit."*
> JOHN 15:2 ESV

## PERSONAL APPLICATION:

Pruning is painful. However, it's also purposeful. If you prune a rosebush, it flourishes and produces beautiful, healthy buds; if you let it run wild, it turns scraggly and misshapen. If you sense you're being pruned, it's not a punishment. It means there's fruit in your life—and God is preparing you for more.

Do you see the hand of Providence—of the Almighty—at work in your life? Take this time to write down some of the "providential" ways God has worked in your life over the years. Reminisce. Reflect. Remember. Think over all the things—the losses and the gains—that seemed like a mistake at the time but have since allowed you to branch out.

## PRAYER FOR TODAY:

*Heavenly Father, thank You for all the providential things You've done in my life over the years. Thank You for giving me what I need and protecting me from what I don't. Please help me to rest in the knowledge of Your wisdom and care in this area of my life. [Add your prayer request.] In Jesus' name, amen.*

---

*"The very hairs of your head are all numbered. Do not fear therefore; you are of more value than many sparrows."*
LUKE 12:7 NKJV

# Day 35
# AS UNTO THE LORD

*Whatever you do, work at it with all your heart,
as working for the Lord, not for human masters.*
COLOSSIANS 3:23 NIV

> "I've done my best and I begin to understand what is meant by the 'joy of the strife.' Next to trying and winning, the best thing is trying and failing." (CH. 35)

In this chapter, Anne spends the school year at Queen's College. She's terribly homesick at first, but weekend trips back to Green Gables help make things easier. After Christmas everyone settles down to study. Anne works "hard and steadily" like always, but a subtle change has come over her: Her studies are no longer centered on her rivalry with Gilbert or on her need to win at everything. Now she's more focused on understanding the "joy of the strife."

Anne no longer wishes "to win for the sake of defeating Gilbert," though she considers him a "worthy foeman" and would be proud of a "well-won victory." She thinks it's "worth while to win" a medal, but she realizes life won't be "insupportable" if she doesn't. Though she sometimes thinks her looming exams mean "everything," when she looks out her window at the buds of spring, her exams "don't seem half so important."

Best of all, Anne is learning to enjoy the journey and give

herself space to breathe. Pleasing Matthew and Marilla is now her main aspiration. She realizes that working hard has its own merits: "Next to trying and winning, the best thing is trying and failing." And she no longer makes herself ill with study. Instead, she makes time for friends and attends church and eats dinner on Sundays with Miss Barry.

It's a wonderful thing to realize you're doing something for the "joy of the strife" and no ulterior motive. There's a unique joy that comes from doing something well for the sake of doing your best. When you work as though you work for God alone, there's a different kind of satisfaction than when you're trying to please others, get ahead, look good, feel good, beat the competition, or prove yourself.

God looks at you differently than the world looks at you: "For the LORD sees not as man sees: man looks on the outward appearance, but the LORD looks on the heart" (1 Samuel 16:7 ESV). When God called the prophet Samuel to go to Jesse's house to anoint a new king, Samuel assumed God wanted to crown one of Jesse's older sons. But God chose David—the youngest of his eight brothers, the lowly shepherd, the least likely candidate— to be king over Israel! Why? Because he looked at David's heart and was pleased with what he saw there.

> *He takes no pleasure in the strength of a horse or in human might. No, the LORD's delight is in those who fear him, those who put their hope in his unfailing love.*
> PSALM 147:10-11 NLT

## PERSONAL APPLICATION:

If you could hear "Well done" from anyone, whom would you want to hear it from most? Whom do you most want to please? If you're feeling discouraged, weary, or burned out, it could be a symptom of people-pleasing. When you work to gain the approval of others, it drains your emotional, spiritual, and physical energy. When you focus on the joy of the strife, your endeavors take on new meaning.

It is impossible to make everyone happy—and you will quickly wear yourself out trying. Remember that God is more pleased with your faith, obedience, and diligence than with your achievements. Your days will start to feel different if you set your mind and heart on working at all you do as unto the Lord.

## PRAYER FOR TODAY:

*Lord, I thank You for this beautiful picture of working for the simple joy of pleasing and glorifying You. I confess that I often work to make other people happy, to avoid criticism, or to prove myself. Working for man's applause makes me weary. Please show me what I need to set down at Your feet today. [Add your prayer request.] In Jesus' name, amen.*

---

*Serve wholeheartedly, as if you were serving the Lord, not people.*
EPHESIANS 6:7 NIV

# Day 36
# CHOSEN

---※---

*Even before he made the world, God loved*
*us and chose us in Christ to be holy*
*and without fault in his eyes.*
EPHESIANS 1:4 NLT

> " 'I'd rather have you than a dozen boys, Anne,' said Matthew patting her hand. 'Just mind you that—rather than a dozen boys. Well now, I guess it wasn't a boy that took the Avery scholarship, was it? It was a girl—my girl—my girl that I'm proud of.' " (CH. 36)

This chapter starts out with so much joy, thankfulness, and hope. Anne finds out she has won the Avery scholarship, and the first thing she wants to do is tell Matthew and Marilla: "Oh, won't Matthew and Marilla be pleased! I must write the news home right away." They travel from Avonlea to attend commencement "with eyes and ears for only one student on the platform."

Back home, however, Anne quickly realizes that things aren't going so well at Green Gables. Matthew's heart is troubling him, there's fear over the bank failing, and Marilla's eyes and headaches are so bad she can't sew or read. Anne wants to do something to make it easier and tells Marilla, "You must take a rest, now that I'm home."

That evening Anne watches Matthew walk slowly with his head bent as he brings up the cows. She says wistfully, "If I had been the boy you sent for. . .I'd be able to help you so much now and spare you in a hundred ways." But Matthew says he'd rather have her than a "dozen boys." He calls her "my girl—my girl that I'm proud of." It's a moment Anne will never forget; she knows without a shadow of a doubt that Matthew only ever wanted her.

You must never forget that you are God's child—his girl, his boy. You're the one He wanted all along. Even "before he made the world," God loved you and chose you "in Christ to be holy and without fault in his eyes" (Ephesians 1:4 NLT). God says to you, dear child, "I have redeemed you; I have called you by name, you are mine" (Isaiah 43:1 ESV).

Your salvation story started before you asked Jesus to be your Savior, before you opened a Bible, went to a church, or learned to say your prayers. His plans for your salvation started before your birth, before your conception, even before He laid the foundations of the earth and "the morning stars sang together and all the angels shouted for joy" (Job 38:7 NLT).

> *You saw me before I was born. Every day of my life was recorded in your book. Every moment was laid out before a single day had passed.*
> PSALM 139:16 NLT

## PERSONAL APPLICATION:

There has never been a moment when God didn't want you. He made you, He chose you, and He gave His only Son for you. He desires to "produce in you, through the power of Jesus Christ, every good thing that is pleasing to him" (Hebrews 13:21 NLT). And He wants you to use your unique gifts and talents to do the "good works" He has prepared for you to do (Ephesians 2:10 NIV).

If you feel like you're not equipped or talented enough to serve God, write this down: "God chose what is foolish in the world to shame the wise; God chose what is weak in the world to shame the strong" (1 Corinthians 1:27 ESV). You don't need to be the best or the brightest; you only need to be willing. You can start by sharing one of today's Bible verses with a friend.

## PRAYER FOR TODAY:

*God, I love You. Thank You for loving me, choosing me, and wanting me. Thank You that You started writing my salvation story before You created the world. I want to grow in confidence as Your child. Help me step out in faith to share Your love with the people around me and discover the good works You have for me to do. [Add your prayer request.] In Jesus' name, amen.*

---

*We are God's handiwork, created in Christ Jesus to do good works, which God prepared in advance for us to do.*
EPHESIANS 2:10 NIV

# Day 37
# SWEET SORROW

---

*Weeping may last through the night,*
*but joy comes with the morning.*
PSALM 30:5 NLT

> *"I love you as dear as if you were my own flesh and blood and you've been my joy and comfort ever since you came to Green Gables."* (CH. 37)

In this chapter, Anne and Marilla lose the most important person in their lives: Matthew Cuthbert. T.he shock of his sudden death catapults Anne into a world of pain and sorrow. She tells Diana, "I want to be quite silent and quiet and try to realize it. I can't realize it." Marilla's grief is "impassioned" and "stormy," but Anne is trapped in a "tearless agony." It seems "a terrible thing" that she cannot cry for Matthew, "whom she had loved so much and who had been so kind to her."

In the middle of night, Anne awakens and finally cries "her heart out." Marilla comes to comfort her, and they cling to one another over their shared sorrow. In this tender moment, Marilla expresses for the first time how much Anne really means to her: "I love you as dear as if you were my own flesh and blood and you've been my joy and comfort ever since you came to Green Gables."

In her sorrow, Anne finds comfort in "the beautiful world

of blossom and love and friendship." When the news spreads, friends and family throng to Green Gables, coming and going "on errands of kindness for the dead and living." The Barrys and Mrs. Lynde remain at Green Gables the first evening, and Diana offers to spend the night.

As the weeks go on, Anne and Marilla stay close to home so neither will feel lonely. Diana visits often, and her "merry words and ways" move Anne to "laughter and smiles." And when Anne feels "something like shame and remorse" that life still has the power to "please her fancy and thrill her heart," Mrs. Allan assures her that Matthew liked to hear her laugh and find "pleasure in the pleasant things" around her. Despite the aching sense of "loss in all familiar things," Anne slowly begins to heal.

When we experience loss, God actively works in invisible and unfathomable ways to comfort us and heal our hearts. He is our "Father of compassion" and "God of all comfort" (2 Corinthians 1:3 NIV). He "heals the brokenhearted" and "binds up their wounds" (Psalm 147:3 NIV). He also sends people—tangible expressions of His love—to sit with us, hug us, cry with us, and pray with us. And He provides everyday moments of "blossom and love and friendship" to help us move forward.

In 1 Thessalonians 4 (NIV), Paul reminded the early church to "encourage one another" in the face of death (v. 18). He said, "Do not grieve like the rest of mankind, who have no hope" (v. 13). In Christ, we'll "be with the Lord forever" in heaven (v. 17). Before ascending into heaven, Jesus gave His faithful followers this promise, "I will come back and take you to be with me that you also may be where I am" (John 14:3 NIV).

*"Blessed are those who mourn, for they shall be comforted."*
MATTHEW 5:4 NKJV

## Personal Application:

Life's greatest sorrows come as a result of losing its greatest gifts and comforts. When we lose someone we love, it feels as though the searing pain will break us into pieces and never cease. In the dark night of our sorrow, we need support, compassion, and comfort.

If you're grieving a loss—whether it's a loved one, a treasured home, or a lifelong dream—take this time to pour out your sorrows before the Lord. Ask Him to heal your broken heart and bind your wounds. If someone you know is grieving, take time this week to minister comfort to them in the same way God has comforted you (2 Corinthians 1:4).

## Prayer for Today:

*God, thank You for being with me through every joy and every sorrow. I lift to You now the pain, the ache, and the loss I feel. Thank You that You care for every single thing that hurts my heart, no matter how big or small. Please heal my brokenness and bind up my wounds. I want to experience another measure of Your healing in this area of my life: [Name the specific area]. In Jesus' name, amen.*

---

*He heals the brokenhearted and binds up their wounds.*
Psalm 147:3 nasb

# Day 38
# NEW LIFE

---※---

*I remain confident of this: I will see the*
*goodness of the LORD in the land of the living.*
PSALM 27:13 NIV

> " 'God's in His heaven, all's right with the world,' whispered Anne softly." (CH. 38)

This final chapter is all about sacrifice, generosity, and new beginnings. It's about the blessing that comes when we choose to give of ourselves to lift up someone we love. After so much pain and heartache following Matthew's death, Anne and Marilla now face new obstacles: Marilla might lose her eyesight—and they might lose Green Gables. At this difficult bend in the road, Anne gives up her future at Redmond College to save Green Gables, and Gilbert Blythe gives up Avonlea school so Anne can teach close to home.

When Anne tells Marilla she has decided to stay home, Marilla listens "like a woman in a dream." Anne is full of "hope and joy" now that she has looked "her duty courageously in the face" and found it "a friend." Marilla tries to voice her concerns, but Anne won't hear of it: "I'm heart glad over the very thought of staying at dear Green Gables. Nobody could love it as you and I do—so we must keep it." Marilla says, "I feel as if you'd given me new life."

Anne feels the same way when she discovers Gilbert gave up Avonlea school for her: "I don't think I ought to let Gilbert make such a sacrifice for—for me." When she thanks him, he asks if they can finally be friends. She confesses that she forgave him "that day by the pond." It's a new beginning for them both. " 'We are going to be the best of friends,' said Gilbert, jubilantly. 'We were born to be good friends, Anne.' "

This book begins and ends with personal sacrifices that produce great blessing. When we stop thinking about what we can *get* and start focusing on what we can *give*, amazing things happen. As we join God in sacrificially loving others, we experience true joy. Our hearts expand when we look our duty "courageously" in the face and find it "a friend." Some of life's best moments occur when we give of ourselves for the good of another.

In the Bible, sacrifice produces new life. From Genesis to Revelation, God reveals His salvation plans for all of humanity. The Bible tells the twisting, turning tale of Jesus' family tree—his ancestors before Him and His followers after Him. It's the story of a heavenly Father who sacrificed His only Son so that you and I could have new life and join His family. It's about Jesus who willingly died for the sins of the world and gave His own life as "the sacrifice that atones for our sins" (1 John 2:2 NLT). He *died* so that you and I might *live*.

*"I came that they may have life and have it abundantly."*
JOHN 10:10 ESV

## Personal Application:

God is calling you to go deeper in your relationship with Him, but there may be something you need to surrender and lay at His feet. If there's anything standing between you and Jesus, He's inviting you to set it down and draw near. Come before Him in humble adoration with outstretched arms and open palms, offering all that you are and all that you have to Him.

When God asks us to set something down, even something really good, it's often because He is preparing us to pick up something even better. If you sense your heavenly Father calling you to make an offering—of your time, your possessions, or your talents—take this time now to pray. Your small gift or gesture could make a world of difference to someone else.

## Prayer for Today:

*Dear Jesus, thank You for the sacrifice You made, that I might have abundant new life. Please show me what I need to set down so I can grow in my faith. I want to put my relationship with You first and think of others before myself. Please cultivate a more selfless spirit in me. [Add your prayer request.] In Jesus' name, amen.*

―――――※―――――

*For the joy set before him he endured the cross, scorning its shame, and sat down at the right hand of the throne of God.*

Hebrews 12:2 niv

# Day 39

# RECONCILED
# (A SPECIAL INVITATION)

---※---

*For if, while we were God's enemies, we were
reconciled to him through the death of his Son,
how much more, having been reconciled,
shall we be saved through his life!*
ROMANS 5:10 NIV

> "I've always kind of wished I'd forgiven him when I had the chance." (CH. 37)

One of the most touching moments at the end of *Anne of Green Gables* is when Anne and Gilbert finally reconcile. Gilbert has offered his friendship to Anne for years—apologizing to her numerous times, encouraging her, giving her gifts, and even rescuing her from nearly drowning.

Even so, every fiber of Anne's being fights against Gilbert for five long years. She wants nothing to do with him. She's angry with him and considers him her enemy. She even imagines that he's teasing and taunting her when he's not. She's so wrapped up in her own pride that she's blinded to his friendly overtures. She grows bitter and makes up her mind to hate him. And when he offers her friendship one last time at the pond, she says, "I shall never be friends with you, Gilbert Blythe; and I don't want to be!"

After that, Gilbert leaves her alone. He stops pressing her. He stops trying to win her over. He gives her space. But then the day comes when he makes a great sacrifice for her. When he gives up the Avonlea school for her, he says, "I was pleased to be able to do you some small service." This "small service" comes at a great cost to him, in the room and board he'll have to pay and the long stretches of time away from home. But even though Anne doesn't deserve anything from him after the way she has treated him, he does it anyway.

Gilbert's sacrifice finally melts the last of the ice around Anne's heart. She realizes then that she forgave him long ago at the pond. She has wished they could be friends for years and regrets pushing him away. She puts out a hand to him, offers her thanks, and finally accepts his friendship. There at the gate, they stand talking for a half hour. When Marilla comments on it, Anne can't believe they talked that long: "It seemed just a few minutes. But, you see, we have five years' lost conversations to catch up with."

It's the same with you and me. We are stubborn and bullheaded about allowing God in. We each have our own bitterness, hang-ups, and bad experiences that hold us back. We listen to everyone and everything before we listen to God. We think we have it figured out. We try to solve our own problems. But at every bend in the road, Jesus is there—beckoning to us and offering reconciliation. And even though we didn't do anything to deserve it, Jesus died for us *while* we were still in rebellion against Him.

> *God demonstrates his own love for us in this:*
> *While we were still sinners, Christ died for us.*
> ROMANS 5:8 NIV

# PERSONAL INVITATION:

The reconciliation between Anne and Gilbert is only a tiny glimpse—a fictional glimpse—into the infinite love of Christ. But there are important spiritual truths for us here. There is One who loves you more than any human could ever love you. He made the ultimate sacrifice for you. He is offering you a new life and a forever home.

If you've lived your whole life apart from Jesus, He's offering His love and salvation to you today—He has been pursuing you and loving you, allowing you to walk your own way, but hoping and waiting all along. He's calling to you today, inviting you to come to Him. He made the ultimate sacrifice so that you might live. All you have to do is say yes and ask Him to be your Lord and Savior. When you do, you'll receive forgiveness of sins and eternal life. Please be reconciled to God today, dear one.

# PRAYER FOR SALVATION:

*Lord Jesus, I want to be a child of God. Please forgive me of all my sins. Thank You for dying on the cross for my sins. Please be my Lord and Savior. I ask You to come into my heart and life right now and make me a new person. I want to live with You forever in heaven. Thank You for loving me. Thank You for saving me. In Jesus' name, amen.*

———————※———————

*"Behold, I stand at the door and knock. If anyone hears My voice and opens the door, I will come in to him and dine with him, and he with Me."*
REVELATION 3:20 NKJV

If you're living estranged from Jesus, if you've walked away from Him, or if you're living in rebellion, today is the day to confess your sins, repent, and turn back to Jesus. God wants to bring you back into the fold, back into fellowship with other believers, and back into a personal, daily relationship with Him. Don't wait any longer. Today is the day. Your heavenly Father is waiting with open arms.

## PRAYER FOR RECONCILIATION:

*Lord Jesus, thank You that You died for me, that You saved me, and that You love me forever. I want to renew my covenant with You today. I confess to You that I've been walking apart from You on my own paths. I've wandered and strayed from Your commandments. I confess to You my sins. [Add your confession here.] Please forgive me and make me new. I want to follow You with my whole heart. In Jesus' name, amen.*

---

*As it is said, "Today, if you hear his voice, do not harden your hearts as in the rebellion."*
HEBREWS 3:15 ESV

If you love and know Jesus but want a renewed relationship with Him, are in need of revival, or find yourself in a dry season, today is the day to ask the Holy Spirit to refresh your body, mind, and soul. Take this time to meet with your Abba, Father and ask Him to speak words of life over you and revive you.

# PRAYER FOR RENEWAL:

*Precious Jesus, I come before You, a worn and weary traveler.
The soil of my spirit is parched and dry. I'm running on empty.
Please, Holy Spirit, water my soul. Wash me anew. Drench me
in Your love. Bring Your rain, oh Lord. Bring refreshment, new
life, tender mercies, and fresh manna. Take me to new heights.
Open my eyes anew to see You face-to-face. And fill my cup
again. I love You, Jesus. In Your name I pray. Amen.*

---

*You gave your good Spirit to instruct them
and did not withhold your manna from their
mouth and gave them water for their thirst.*
NEHEMIAH 9:20 ESV

# SPECIAL NOTE:

If you prayed to receive Christ as your Savior today, hallelujah!
All of heaven is rejoicing (Luke 15:7)! You are now—and will
forever be—a child of God. Be sure to tell someone about the
good news of your adoption in Christ! And make sure you connect with a local Christian church so you can grow in your new
relationship with Christ.

If you prayed any of today's prayers, please send me a note
at RachelDodge.com. I would love to hear your story and pray
for you!

# Day 40
# The Story of
# Anne's Birth

---

*There is an appointed time for everything.*
ECCLESIASTES 3:1 NASB

> "Elderly couple apply to orphan asylum for a boy. By mistake a girl is sent them."[1]

Lucy Maud ("without an *e*") Montgomery jotted down those two sentences in her writer's notebook in 1895. At the time, it was just another brainstorm for one of her many short stories. Ten long years passed before Maud revisited the idea. When she did, she wrote *Anne of Green Gables*—a novel that has since touched millions of hearts all around the world.

When Maud came back to the little orphan girl who was sent "by mistake," she thought the idea would make a perfect seven-chapter serial for a Sunday school paper. She named the girl Anne Shirley, gave her red hair, and made her "outspoken and imaginative."[2] But as Anne began to "take on a life of her own," Maud soon realized that a short story wasn't enough. As biographer Catherine M. Andronik attests, "A character like Anne demanded more than just a few pages. She demanded a whole novel."[3]

One spring evening in 1905, as she perched on the edge of

her grandmother's kitchen table with her feet on the sofa, Maud began writing *Anne of Green Gables*. When she finished writing it, she sent the manuscript to several publishers and waited expectantly for their answers. Unfortunately, every publisher rejected it. Maud gave up, stashed the story in a hatbox, and went back to her other work.

A year later, on a serendipitous trip to the attic, Maud came across the hatbox. She read Anne's story again and decided it was *good*! She made revisions and sent it out again—this time to the L. C. Page Publishing Company. Within two months, they replied with an offer to publish. *Anne of Green Gables* was released in 1908 and became an instant bestseller.

To date, *Anne of Green Gables* has sold more than 50 million copies and has been translated into at least 36 languages. During her lifetime (November 30, 1874–April 24, 1942), L. M. Montgomery, OBE, "Officer of the Order of the British Empire," published 20 novels (including an entire series of Anne books), 530 short stories, 500 poems, and 30 essays.[4]

Maud enjoyed a successful writing career and created a beautiful legacy with her gift of writing. Her books make us laugh, they make us cry, and they give us hope. Best of all, they remind us that "kindred spirits are not so scarce" as we might think.

---

*Anne of Green Gables* has lifted people's spirits for generations—and it all started with two short sentences hastily scribbled in a notebook. Let this be a reminder to you that God is still writing your story. His plans are unfolding all around you. He has a vision for your future. He sees around the bend in the road and past the horizon.

God also has a story for you to tell—the unique story of

your spiritual adoption into His forever family. You see, God is calling you to be an orphan-finder and an introduction-maker. He's asking you to be a Marilla and a Matthew, a Diana and a Gilbert, a Mrs. Allan and a Miss Stacy. He's asking you to live like Anne—full of life, spirit, and love. He's asking you to wrap your arms around the brokenhearted people all around you and lead them to the cross.

1. Catherine M. Andronik, *Kindred Spirit: A Biography of L. M. Montgomery, Creator of Anne of Green Gables* (New York: Atheneum, 1993), 73.
2. Andronik, 73.
3. Andronik, 74.
4. L. M. Montgomery, "Lucy Maud Montgomery Biography," in *The Alpine Path (Annotated): The Story of My Career* (1917; repr., San Bernadino, CA: CreateSpace, 1998), 1.

# Author's Note

I pray that this devotional book has provided a healing balm for your soul, kindred spirit. I hope it has increased your understanding of God's deep love for you and your place of belonging in His forever family. Never forget that you belong to Jesus—you are a child of God!

If you've enjoyed reading this book, I hope you'll share it with your kindred spirit friends and family. You might even want to invite your bosom friend(s) over for tea to discuss it together. If you do, I hope you'll decorate your table with an abundance of wild roses and delicate ferns, flavor your cake with *vanilla*, and make up a fresh batch of raspberry cordial for those who prefer it to currant wine.

I'd love to connect with you! You can find me online at Rachel Dodge.com to read my blog or link to my @KindredSpiritBooks Instagram account and my Facebook author page.

May the Lord bless you and keep you always!

# DISCUSSION QUESTIONS

*"Where two or three gather in my name, there am I with them."*
MATTHEW 18:20 NIV

Note to parents: To access the supplemental application questions I've designed especially for kids, please visit www.Rachel Dodge.com/anneforkids.

If you're discussing this devotional with a friend, family member, or group, be sure to open with prayer. The following questions can help facilitate deeper discussion when needed. You can also use these questions for personal reflection or journaling. Enjoy!

## DAY 1
What kinds of detours or delays are you experiencing?
How do you react to unexpected changes?
How has a past detour led to something good?

## DAY 2
Who in your life is a good listener?
Are you able to talk to God like a loving father?
Whom do you know who needs someone to listen?

## DAY 3
In what ways do you relate to Anne in this chapter?
When have you felt rejected before?
Which Bible verse(s) from today's reading speaks to your heart?

## Day 4

Who in your life has spoken up on your behalf?

How does Matthew's example help you better understand God's love for you?

What does the phrase "child of God" mean to you?

## Day 5

What are you waiting on right now?

What makes waiting and stillness so difficult?

How is God speaking to you as you wait?

## Day 6

In what ways can you relate to Anne in this chapter?

Do you feel like you're sitting next to God or across the room from Him right now?

Where do you need Jesus to intervene in your life or in the life of a friend or family member?

## Day 7

Where is your ideal place to pray?

What step of faith do you want to take this month?

Read Zechariah 4:10. What do you think God wants to say to you through this verse?

## Day 8

When have you felt like an outsider?

Where or with whom do you feel like you belong?

Someone in your life needs an invitation to coffee, church, or dinner. Who is it?

## Day 9

What old scars are you carrying?

What are some names or labels you've been given?

What new name in Christ do you want to meditate on this week?

## Day 10

Who has hurt you? Have you forgiven him or her?

Whom have you hurt? Have you asked for forgiveness?

What step is God asking you to take toward reconciliation?

## Day 11

Where is your quiet place where you meet with God?

What would help you grow in your personal prayer life?

Make a date to "come away" with Jesus this week and mark it on your calendar!

## Day 12

Who are your bosom friends?

In what ways is God calling you to be a better friend?

What is your prayer regarding friendship?

## Day 13

Where do you sense discouragement in this "sowing" season?

Where have you seen fruit in past years?

What is God teaching you about sacred moments?

## Day 14

What relationship issues are you facing?

What do you think God is asking you to do?

If you have a difficult relationship with someone, will you

commit to set a reminder and pray for that person each day for the next thirty days?

## Day 15

In what ways can you relate to Anne's shame, anger, and humiliation?
Do you sense a hardened heart toward someone who has hurt you?
What will it take for you to move forward?

## Day 16

What battle(s) are raging around you?
What Bible verse from today's reading encouraged you?
Write one down and carry it with you.
What is your prayer when you're in the midst of a difficult trial?

## Day 17

Share a story of God's faithfulness. What streams has He provided in your desert?
How is God encouraging your heart right now?
What burden(s) do you want to cast into God's hands?

## Day 18

In what ways do you see God equipping you for the work He has given you to do?
What are you asking God to work together for good?
How has God used your past experiences to help someone in your present life?

## Day 19

Would you describe yourself as courageous or timid?

In what area of your life is God asking you to be brave?
How can you prepare your heart for a step of faith?

## Day 20
Would you say you live like an orphan or like you belong to Jesus?
How did you live before you met Jesus? How do you live now?
Where do you want to grow?

## Day 21
Have you ever had a liniment cake–type situation?
Tell about a time when you experienced God's new mercies.
In what part of your life do you need a fresh start?

## Day 22
Who are your mentors?
Do you know of someone who needs a mentor?
Take time to pray and ask God to open the door if you're missing either one.

## Day 23
Describe a ridgepole moment you've experienced.
Are you walking on spiritual solid ground or on shifting sand?
What do you need to do to walk on God's paths more consistently?

## Day 24
How would you describe your personal school of faith?
What's going well? What needs more attention?
What would help you gain regularity and smoothness in your walk with God?

## Day 25

What is one of the greatest gifts someone has given you?
Who is good at noticing your needs?
How have you experienced God's fatherly love recently?

## Day 26

In what area(s) do you want to cultivate everyday faithfulness?
What mundane parts of life are a struggle for you?
What small deposits are you making to grow your relationship with God?

## Day 27

What are you most sensitive or self-conscious about?
Where do you think your sensitivity comes from?
Are you ready to pray and ask God to open your eyes to your blind spots and heal old wounds?

## Day 28

Are you holding a grudge against someone? Think carefully.
In what ways does bitterness affect your relationships?
Are you ready to pray for a soft, forgiving heart?

## Day 29

Where do you feel most at home?
In what area of ministry do you feel called to serve?
Why do you think God has planted you where you are today?

## Day 30

What people form your circle of personal influencers?
What other people influence you through what you watch, read, and listen to?

Rate your influencers. Are there any that diminish your interest in pursuing God?

## Day 31

Would you say you have a gentle, quiet spirit?
What activity or environment helps you enter into quiet reflection?
What do you need to do to nourish and feed your soul today?

## Day 32

Do you find it harder to rejoice with those who rejoice or weep with those who weep?
Why do you think one is easier or harder than the other?
Who in your life is always there to rejoice and weep with you?

## Day 33

What or who causes you to feel like you're missing out?
When do you tend to experience discontentment?
What or who helps you focus on your eternal riches in Christ?

## Day 34

Where do you see God pruning you?
What areas of your life are blooming?
In what ways do you see the Almighty at work in providential ways in your life?

## Day 35

How did you answer the questions in today's personal application section?
How hard is it for you to work unto the Lord and not for human applause?

What burdens are you carrying that God hasn't asked you to carry?

## Day 36

What verses from today's reading encouraged your heart?
Do you ever struggle to believe you're loved or wanted by God?
What good works has God called you to do?

## Day 37

How have you seen God work in your life in times of sorrow?
What comforts you most when you're grieving or struggling with loss or change?
Is there someone you know who needs comfort?

## Day 38

Why do you think sacrifice is so powerful?
Who has made sacrifices for you?
What touches you most about Christ's sacrifice for you?

## Day 39

Did you pray one of the prayers? If so, which one?
In what ways does the concept of reconciliation speak to your heart?
What next steps do you want to take in your faith journey?

## Day 40

Where do you see God's fingerprints on the story of your life?
Which *Anne of Green Gables* character inspires you most?
How can you live more like that person did in the book?
With whom is God asking you to share your salvation story?

# THE WORLD ACCORDING to Anne Shirley
## A Glossary

Anne Shirley is one of the most quotable characters in literature! While space won't allow for an exhaustive list, the following is a humorous and heartfelt collection of some of Anne's most memorable sayings broken down by subject.

## ADOPTION

- Oh, it seems so wonderful that I'm going to live with you and belong to you. (ch. 2)

- It gives me that pleasant ache again just to think of coming to a really truly home. (ch. 2)

- It's a million times nicer to be Anne of Green Gables than Anne of nowhere in particular, isn't it? (ch. 8)

## APOLOGIES

- I thought since I had to [apologize] I might as well do it thoroughly. (ch. 10)

- Oh, Mrs. Barry, please forgive me. I did not mean to—to—intoxicate Diana. (ch. 16)

- It gives you a lovely, comfortable feeling to apologize and be forgiven, doesn't it? (ch. 10)

🌢 I've had practice in confessing, fortunately. (ch. 19)

🌢 What a stubborn little goose I was. I've been—I may as well make a complete confession—I've been sorry ever since. (ch. 38)

## BEAUTY

🌢 It's bad enough to have red hair myself, but I positively couldn't endure it in a bosom friend. (ch. 8)

🌢 Have you ever imagined what it must feel like to be divinely beautiful? (ch. 2)

🌢 Next to being beautiful oneself—and that's impossible in my case—it would be best to have a beautiful bosom friend. (ch. 8)

🌢 I'd rather be pretty than clever. (ch. 15)

## BLOOMS AND BOUGHS

🌢 It would be lovely to sleep in a wild cherry-tree all white with bloom in the moonshine, don't you think? (ch. 2)

🌢 I read in a book once that a rose by any other name would smell as sweet, but I've never been able to believe it. I don't believe a rose would be as nice if it was called a thistle or a skunk cabbage. (ch. 5)

🌢 Can I take the apple blossoms with me for company? (ch. 8)

- Oh, look, here's a big bee just tumbled out of an apple blossom. Just think what a lovely place to live—in an apple blossom! Fancy going to sleep in it when the wind was rocking it. If I wasn't a human girl I think I'd like to be a bee and live among the flowers. (ch. 8)

- "Oh, Marilla," she exclaimed one Saturday morning, coming dancing in with her arms full of gorgeous boughs, "I'm so glad I live in a world where there are Octobers. It would be terrible if we just skipped from September to November, wouldn't it?" (ch. 16)

- Look at these maple branches. Don't they give you a thrill—several thrills? (ch. 16)

- I'm so sorry for people who live in lands where there are no Mayflowers. (ch. 20)

# BOOKS

- "My life is a perfect graveyard of buried hopes." That's a sentence I read in a book once, and I say it over to comfort myself whenever I'm disappointed in anything. (ch. 5)

- Don't you just love poetry that gives you a crinkly feeling up and down your back? (ch. 5)

- That was a thrilling book, Marilla. The heroine had five lovers. I'd be satisfied with one, wouldn't you? (ch. 8)

- Long ago, before I had ever seen a diamond, I read about them and I tried to imagine what they would be like. (ch. 13)

- I won't allow myself to open that new book Jane lent me until I'm through. But it's a terrible temptation, Matthew. (ch. 18)

- I love a book that makes me cry. (ch. 18)

- It's so much more romantic to end a story up with a funeral than a wedding. (ch. 26)

# CHILDREN

- I'm better at looking after children, though. I've had so much experience at that. It's such a pity you haven't any here for me to look after. (ch. 4)

- I like babies in moderation, but twins three times in succession is too much. (ch. 5)

- People who have to look after twins can't be expected to say their prayers. (ch. 7)

# COOKING

- I never thought about that pie from the moment I put it in the oven till now, although I felt instinctively that there was something missing on the dinner table. (ch. 20)

- I shall always be pointed at as the girl who flavored a cake with anodyne liniment. (ch. 21)

- The tears just rained down over my cheeks while I mixed the cake. But I forgot the flour and the cake was a dismal failure. (ch. 16)

- Yes; but cakes have such a terrible habit of turning out bad just when you especially want them to be good. (ch. 21)

- There's so little scope for imagination in cookery. You just have to go by rules. (ch. 16)

- Diana, fancy if you can my extreme horror at finding a mouse drowned in that pudding sauce! (ch. 16)

## DREAMS

- Dreams don't often come true, do they? (ch. 2)

- One can dream so much better in a room where there are pretty things. (ch. 16)

- My dimple-dream will never come true; but so many of my dreams have that I mustn't complain. (ch. 33)

- Oh, it's delightful to have ambitions. I'm so glad I have such a lot. (ch. 34)

- I'm just going to take this one day off to visit all the dear old spots and hunt up my old dreams, and then it will be your turn to be lazy while I do the work. (ch. 36)

## FASHION

- Redheaded people can't wear pink, not even in imagination. (ch. 5)

- It would give me such a thrill, Marilla, just to wear a dress with puffed sleeves. (ch. 11)

🌿 I'm so glad that puffed sleeves are still fashionable. It did seem to me that I'd never get over it if they went out before I had a dress with them. (ch. 25)

🌿 Do you suppose it's wrong for us to think so much about our clothes? Marilla says it is very sinful. But it is such an interesting subject, isn't it? (ch. 29)

🌿 It is ever so much easier to be good if your clothes are fashionable. (ch. 29)

# FOOD

🌿 I can't. I'm in the depths of despair. Can you eat when you are in the depths of despair? (ch. 3)

🌿 Breakfast seems so commonplace at such an exciting moment. (ch. 25)

🌿 I love bright red drinks, don't you? They taste twice as good as any other color. (ch. 16)

🌿 Boiled pork and greens are so unromantic when one is in affliction. (ch. 14)

# FRIENDSHIP

🌿 A bosom friend—an intimate friend, you know—a really kindred spirit to whom I can confide my inmost soul. (ch. 8)

🌿 "Oh, Diana," said Anne at last, clasping her hands and speaking almost in a whisper, "oh, do you think you can like me a little—enough to be my bosom friend?" (ch. 7)

🍂 Just imagine if you were a poor little orphan girl that kind people had adopted and you had just one bosom friend in all the world. (ch. 16)

🍂 "Ten minutes isn't very long to say an eternal farewell in," said Anne tearfully. "Oh, Diana, will you promise faithfully never to forget me, the friend of your youth, no matter what dearer friends may caress thee?" (ch. 17)

🍂 I'm always getting into scrapes myself and getting my best friends—people I'd shed my heart's blood for—into them too. (ch. 19)

🍂 It's as good as an extra conscience to have a minister's wife for your friend. (ch. 29)

🍂 But when I have such good friends as you and Matthew and Mrs. Allan and Miss Stacy I ought to grow up successfully, and I'm sure it will be my own fault if I don't. (ch. 31)

## HOMEMAKING

🍂 I cannot tie myself down to anything so unromantic as dishwashing at this thrilling moment. (ch. 18)

🍂 I didn't know I starched the handkerchiefs. All the time I was ironing I was trying to think of a name for a new island Diana and I have discovered up the brook. (ch. 20)

🍂 I think some kinds of sewing would be nice; but there's no scope for imagination in patchwork. (ch. 13)

&#x2741; I wish time went as quick sewing patches as it does when I'm playing with Diana, though. (ch. 8)

## IMAGINATION

&#x2741; It's delightful when your imaginations come true, isn't it? (ch. 2)

&#x2741; But I just went to work and imagined that I had on the most beautiful pale blue silk dress—because when you are imagining you might as well imagine something worth while—and a big hat all flowers and nodding plumes, and a gold watch, and kid gloves and boots. (ch. 2)

&#x2741; Now I'm going to imagine things into this room so that they'll always stay imagined. (ch. 8)

&#x2741; Oh, there's so much scope for imagination in a wind! (ch. 10)

&#x2741; I suppose the minister had to match it to the text. I didn't think he was a bit interesting. The trouble with him seems to be that he hasn't enough imagination. (ch. 11)

## KINDRED SPIRITS

&#x2741; I felt that [Matthew] was a kindred spirit as soon as ever I saw him. (ch. 4)

&#x2741; Matthew and I are such kindred spirits I can read his thoughts without words at all. (ch. 18)

&#x2741; I would like to, because you seem like an interesting lady, and you might even be a kindred spirit although you don't look very much like it. (ch. 19)

- Kindred spirits are not so scarce as I used to think. It's splendid to find out there are so many of them in the world. (ch. 19)

## LIFELONG SORROWS

- I know it is just plain red and it breaks my heart. It will be my lifelong sorrow. (ch. 2)

- It's all very well to read about sorrows and imagine yourself living through them heroically, but it's not so nice when you really come to have them, is it? (ch. 4)

- Oh, Mrs. Lynde, please, please, forgive me. If you refuse it will be a lifelong sorrow on a poor little orphan girl. (ch. 10)

- I don't feel that I could endure the disappointment if anything happened to prevent me from getting to the picnic. I suppose I'd live through it, but I'm certain it would be a lifelong sorrow. (ch. 13)

## MISTAKES

- I make so many mistakes. But then just think of all the mistakes I don't make, although I might. (ch. 19)

- Marilla, isn't it nice to think that tomorrow is a new day with no mistakes in it yet? (ch. 21)

- ⚘ I never make the same mistake twice. (ch. 21)

- ⚘ There must be a limit to the mistakes one person can make, and when I get to the end of them, then I'll be through with them. That's a very comforting thought. (ch. 21)

- ⚘ Ever since I came to Green Gables I've been making mistakes, and each mistake has helped to cure me of some great shortcoming. (ch. 28)

## NAMES (PEOPLE AND PLACES)

- ⚘ When I don't like the name of a place or a person I always imagine a new one and always think of them so. (ch. 2)

- ⚘ But they shouldn't call that lovely place the Avenue. There is no meaning in a name like that. They should call it—let me see—the White Way of Delight. (ch. 2)

- ⚘ I shall call it—let me see—the Lake of Shining Waters. Yes, that is the right name for it. I know because of the thrill. (ch. 2)

- ⚘ Will you please call me Cordelia? (ch. 3)

- ⚘ But if you call me Anne please call me Anne spelled with an *e*. (ch. 3)

- ⚘ Oh, I like things to have handles even if they are only geraniums. It makes them seem more like people. (ch. 4)

- ⚘ I named that cherry-tree outside my bedroom window this morning. I called it Snow Queen because it was so white. (ch. 4)

- We have agreed to call the spring down by the log bridge the Dryad's Bubble. (ch. 12)

- We call it Idlewild. Isn't that a poetical name? (ch. 13)

- Oh, we have named that little round pool over in Mr. Barry's field Willowmere. I got that name out of the book Diana lent me. (ch. 13)

# PRAYER

- Mr. Bell made an awfully long prayer. I would have been dreadfully tired before he got through if I hadn't been sitting by that window. (ch. 11)

- Why must people kneel down to pray? If I really wanted to pray I'll tell you what I'd do. I'd go out into a great big field all alone or in the deep, deep woods and I'd look up into the sky—up-up-up—into that lovely blue sky that looks as if there was no end to its blueness. And then I'd just feel a prayer. (ch. 7)

- Gracious heavenly Father—that's the way the ministers say it in church, so I suppose it's all right in private prayer, isn't it? (ch. 7)

- You couldn't really expect a person to pray very well the first time she tried, could you? (ch. 8)

- I thought out a splendid prayer after I went to bed, just as I promised you I would. It was nearly as long as a minister's and so poetical. (ch. 8)

- Oh, Marilla, it was like a beautiful dream! It gave me a thrill and I just said, "Thank you for it, God," two or three times. (ch. 11)

- "Yours respectfully, Anne Shirley." (ch. 7)

# ROMANCE

- I am so fond of romantic things, and a graveyard full of buried hopes is about as romantic a thing as one can imagine isn't it? (ch. 5)

- It would have been such a romantic experience to have been nearly drowned. (ch. 14)

- And Anne is such an unromantic name. (ch. 3)

- Going around by the main road would have been so unromantic. (ch. 15)

- "Thou" and "thee" seem so much more romantic than "you." (ch. 17)

- A haunted wood is so very romantic, Marilla. (ch. 20)

- I don't believe I'd really want to be a sensible person, because they are so unromantic. (ch. 26)

- I have come to the conclusion that it is no use trying to be romantic in Avonlea. (ch. 28)

# THRILLS

- When I hit on a name that suits exactly it gives me a thrill. (ch. 2)

- Mrs. Barry had the very best china set out, Marilla, just as if I was real company. I can't tell you what a thrill it gave me. (ch. 18)

- That is the first time I was ever called "Miss." Such a thrill as it gave me! (ch. 22)

- I just tremble when I think of it, but it's a nice thrilly kind of tremble. (ch. 24)

- Oh, Diana, will we really see our names in print? It makes me thrill to think of it. (ch. 25)

- I'd love to go up in a balloon, Marilla; it would be simply thrilling. (ch. 29)

- I'd love to be able to faint, wouldn't you, Marilla? (ch. 13)

## TREES

- "Listen to the trees talking in their sleep," she whispered, as he lifted her to the ground. "What nice dreams they must have!" (ch. 2)

- "Maples are such sociable trees," said Anne; "they're always rustling and whispering to you." (ch. 15)

- Those trees look as if I could blow them away with a breath—pouf! I'm so glad I live in a world where there are white frosts, aren't you? (ch. 18)

# VOWS

- Oh, Diana, will you promise faithfully never to forget me, the friend of your youth, no matter what dearer friends may caress thee? (ch. 17)

- Of course I promised Diana that no Queen's girl, no matter how much I liked her, should ever be as dear to me as she is; but I've lots of second-best affections to bestow. (ch. 34)

- I solemnly swear to be faithful to my bosom friend, Diana Barry, as long as the sun and moon shall endure. (ch. 12)

# WISDOM

- It's been my experience that you can nearly always enjoy things if you make up your mind firmly that you will. (ch. 5)

- It's all very well to read about sorrows and imagine yourself living through them heroically, but it's not so nice when you really come to have them, is it? (ch. 9)

- "Oh, Marilla, looking forward to things is half the pleasure of them," exclaimed Anne. "You mayn't get the things themselves; but nothing can prevent you from having the fun of looking forward to them." (ch. 13)

- But really, Marilla, one can't stay sad very long in such an interesting world, can one? (ch. 17)

- "The best of it all was the coming home." (ch. 29)

- It's nicer to think dear, pretty thoughts and keep them in one's heart, like treasures. (ch. 31)

- Next to trying and winning, the best thing is trying and failing. (ch. 35)

- I shall give life here my best, and I believe it will give its best to me in return. (ch. 38)

## WORDS

- And people laugh at me because I use big words. But if you have big ideas you have to use big words to express them, haven't you? (ch. 2)

- Words fail me to describe that ice cream. (ch. 14)

- When I'm grown up, I'm always going to talk to little girls as if they were too, and I'll never laugh when they use big words. (ch. 18)

- In two more years I'll be really grown up. It's a great comfort to think that I'll be able to use big words then without being laughed at. (ch. 26)

- "I'm just dazzled inside," said Anne. "I want to say a hundred things, and I can't find words to say them in." (ch. 32)

# ACKNOWLEDGMENTS

I must start by thanking my Lord and Savior Jesus Christ for the immense privilege of writing this book. It is my sacrifice of praise, my jar of perfume poured out at His feet.

A book like this doesn't happen without an entire "Avonlea" full of wonderful people to help, cheer, and encourage all along the way. I extend my deepest thanks to the following people:

Janet Grant of Books & Such Literary Management for representing me, believing in me, and helping make my writing dreams a reality! I am continually grateful to God for introducing us—thank you for sharing your wisdom, time, and experience with me.

Everyone at Barbour Publishing who helped make this beautiful book possible. Thank you to Annie Tipton for catching the vision of this devotional and allowing me to write the book that's been on my heart for so many years.

Jana Christy for her beautiful illustrations. Thank you for bringing Anne and her family and friends to life! I fell in love with Anne all over again when I saw her walking across the front cover of my very own book.

My bosom friends Courtney Boudreau and Tammy Gurzhiy for their unflagging support of this project from the very beginning and their firm belief in what God has called me to do.

My friend and fellow author Shauna Pilgreen. You inspire, challenge, and motivate me. Our weekly Marco Polo chats keep me grounded and excited about this writing life!

My writing circle friends: Helen Arnold, Rosie Makinney, and Holly Varni. God brought you into my life at just the right time.

My faithful friends and prayer warriors: Meghan Clark, Valerie Cimino, Leann Crutchfield, Carolyn Frank, Hennie McIntire, Krissy Miller, Taylre Nelson, Kristi Rapoza, and Jenice Williams. Thank you for your love and encouragement through every season of life.

My fabulous beta readers: Tammy Gurzhiy, Krissy Miller, Lauren Miller, Katie Kuhl, Kristi Rapoza, Kristina Van Coops, and Holly Varni.

My brother, Matthew Beckman, for being my first (and forever) bosom friend.

My dad, George Beckman, for being a faithful (and fast) first reader. I can always count on you to give me great notes.

My parents, George and Ruth Beckman, for introducing me to Anne in the first place. Thank you for teaching me to love great books and for giving me space to dream and grow. You're the best and most loving Matthew and Marilla a sensitive and imaginative girl could ever want.

My children, Lizzy and Jack, for loving me and supporting my writing work. Your prayers, back rubs, and funny antics make my days sunny. I'm so proud of you both.

And my husband, Bobby, for his generous and passionate support of my highest ideals and filmiest dreams. You are my bosom friend, my kindred spirit, my Matthew, and my Gilbert all wrapped in one. Thank you for the many hours, months, days, and nights you invested in this project—encouraging and praying, reading and verse checking—it wouldn't have been possible without you. I love you!

Finally, I extend my deepest thanks to L.M. Montgomery for the gift of this beautiful novel, without which none of this would be possible, and to the Heirs of L.M. Montgomery for their commitment to preserving the enduring legacy of her life and works.

# BIBLIOGRAPHY

*Anne of Green Gables* by L.M. Montgomery is in the public domain. All quotations are taken from the Project Gutenberg edition: Montgomery, L.M. *Anne of Green Gables* (1908). Urbana, Illinois: Project Gutenberg, 1992.

Andronik, Catherine M. *Kindred Spirit: A Biography of L. M. Montgomery, Creator of Anne of Green Gables*. New York: Atheneum, 1993.

Browning, Robert. *Pippa Passes* (1841). Urbana, IL: Project Gutenberg, 2016.

Montgomery, L. M. *Anne of Green Gables* (1908). Urbana, IL: Project Gutenberg, 1992.

———. "Lucy Maud Montgomery Biography." In *The Alpine Path (Annotated): The Story of My Career* (1917). San Bernadino, CA: CreateSpace, 1998.

# ABOUT THE AUTHOR

Rachel Dodge teaches college writing and literature classes, speaks at libraries, book clubs, and reading groups, and is the author of *Praying with Jane: 31 Days Through the Prayers of Jane Austen*. She is passionate about encouraging and equipping families to grow closer to Jesus through prayer, devotional time, and Bible study. A true kindred spirit at heart, Rachel loves puffed sleeves, classic books, and historic homes and gardens. She makes her home in California with her husband and two children. You can visit her online at RachelDodge.com.

# Scripture Index

OLD TESTAMENT